## DATE DUE

| | | | |
|---|---|---|---|
| | | | |
| | | | |
| | | | |
| | | | |
| | | | |
| | | | |
| | | | |
| | | | |
| | | | |
| | | | |
| | | | |
| | | | |
| | | | |
| | | | |
| | | | |
| | | | |

DEMCO 38-296

# GREAT WRITERS OF THE ENGLISH LANGUAGE

# *Exotic Journeys*

# STAFF CREDITS

**Executive Editor**
Reg Wright

**Series Editor**
Sue Lyon

**Editors**
Jude Welton
Sylvia Goulding

**Deputy Editors**
Alice Peebles
Theresa Donaghey

**Features Editors**
Geraldine McCaughrean
Emma Foa
Ian Chilvers

**Art Editors**
Kate Sprawson
Jonathan Alden
Helen James

**Designers**
Simon Wilder
Frank Landamore

**Senior Picture Researchers**
Julia Hanson
Vanessa Fletcher
Georgina Barker

**Picture Clerk**
Vanessa Cawley

**Production Controllers**
Judy Binning
Tom Helsby

**Editorial Secretaries**
Fiona Bowser
Sylvia Osborne

**Managing Editor**
Alan Ross

**Editorial Consultant**
Maggi McCormick

**Publishing Manager**
Robert Paulley

**Reference Edition Published 1989**
Published by Marshall Cavendish Corporation
147 West Merrick Road
Freeport, Long Island
N.Y. 11520

Typeset by Litho Link Ltd., Welshpool
Printed and Bound in Italy by
L.E.G.O. S.p.a. Vicenza

**LIBRARY OF CONGRESS**
**Library of Congress Cataloging-in-Publication Data**
**Great Writers of the English Language**
        p. cm.
        Includes index vol.
        ISBN 1-85435-000-5 (set): $399.95
        1. English literature — History and criticism. 2. English
literature — Stories, plots, etc. 3. American literature — History
and criticism. 4. American literature — Stories, plots, etc.
5. Authors. English — Biography. 6. Authors. American — Biography.
I. Marshall Cavendish Corporation.
PR85.G66 1989
820'.9 – dc19                                                      88-21077
                                                                          CIP

ISBN 1–85435–000–5 (set)
ISBN 1–85435–009–9 (vol)

GREAT WRITERS OF THE ENGLISH LANGUAGE

# *Exotic Journeys*

Charles Darwin

Herman Melville

Joseph Conrad

E. M. Forster

MARSHALL CAVENDISH · NEW YORK · TORONTO · LONDON · SYDNEY

# CONTENTS

# CHARLES DARWIN

## *1809-1882*

From the secluded calm of his country home, the reclusive semi-invalid
Charles Darwin unleashed upon the world ideas that rocked Victorian
society and shook the very foundations of the Christian church – ideas that
provoked some of the most bitter scientific debates ever heard. Even today,
the storm of controversy raised by the publication of *The Origin of Species*
and Darwin's theory of evolution by natural selection is far from over.
The germ of this revolutionary theory had been sown 20 years before –
during a voyage around the world he had made as a young naturalist.

# The Quiet Revolutionary

**After an adventurous youth, Darwin devoted his life to his family and to research. Unwittingly, this gentle scientist became the focus of the greatest controversy of all time.**

A more unlikely revolutionary than Charles Darwin is hard to imagine. Humble, kindly and thoroughly respectable, Darwin's only real passion in life was for natural history. As a young man, he embarked on what was to be a momentous voyage round the world, but then, a few years after his return, he retreated to a secluded house in the Kent countryside. There he remained almost continuously until his death 40 years later, living quietly with his large, adoring family, tending to his plants, carrying out research, and writing.

There was hardly a hint of the battles to come in the easy tranquillity of Darwin's childhood. Born on 12 February 1809 in a house called The Mount, overlooking the River Severn near Shrewsbury, Charles was the fifth of six children. His mother Susannah was the accomplished daughter of the great pottery magnate Josiah Wedgwood. Darwin remembered little of her, for she died when he was barely eight, but his family remained close to her brother, also called Josiah – the association was to be significant. But it was his father Robert Darwin who dominated The Mount.

A dour but widely respected and wealthy physician, Dr Robert Darwin was a gigantic man, like his famous naturalist and philosopher father Erasmus Darwin, weighing almost 24 stone. His children, who loved him dearly, used to say that when he came home in the evening it was like the tide coming in. The Darwin children's chatter always abated when their father rolled in, and the atmosphere at The Mount tended to be a little restrained. But it was a happy home, and Charles' childhood there was comfortable and secure, with ample time to indulge his passion for collecting pebbles, plants and birds' eggs.

As a boy, Charles had a tendency to fib – an odd contrast to his unimpeachable integrity in later years. For example, he once claimed that he could grow different coloured crocuses by watering them with coloured water. But his exaggerations were no more than youthful exuberance. His particular obsession was for hunting beetles, and he and his second cousin William Darwin Fox went to great lengths to capture unusual species. Once, he later recalled, 'I saw two rare beetles and seized one in each hand; then I saw a third and new kind, which I could not bear to lose, so I popped the one which I held in my right hand into my mouth. Alas it ejected some intensely acrid fluid, which burnt my tongue so that I was forced to spit the beetle out.'

Charles was a healthy, affable youth, always out walking, riding or hunting with his cousins, and dashing up to Staffordshire to see Uncle Josiah and his daughters Emma and Fanny in their home at Maer Hall. But there were few signs of academic distinction. Determined that his son should follow a career, Robert

## Key Dates

**1809** Born near Shrewsbury

**1825** Goes to Edinburgh University

**1827** Enters Christ's College, Cambridge

**1831** Joins *HMS Beagle*

**1839** Marries Emma Wedgwood

**1842** Moves to Down House, Kent

**1858** Ideas of Wallace and Darwin presented at Linnaean Society

**1859** *Origin of Species*

**1871** *Descent of Man* published

**1882** Dies at Down House

Mary Evans Picture Library/inset: Royal College of Surgeons, Down House

Darwin sent Charles to Edinburgh University to study medicine in 1825. But Charles was not cut out to be a doctor. Anaesthetics had yet to be invented, and the two operations that he witnessed – one an amputation on a child – made him feel so sick that he had to rush out. The lectures he liked little better, remembering only 'cold breakfastless hours on the properties of rhubarb'. So he occupied his 18 months in Edinburgh looking for shellfish in the Forth, learning to stuff animals, and shooting.

### LOOKING FOR A CAREER

If Charles was not to be a doctor, Robert proposed that he should become a clergyman and, in autumn 1827, the 18-year-old Darwin was sent off to Cambridge. But he was no more keen on his studies here than he had been in Edinburgh and, in his own words, 'continued to collect insects, hunt, shoot & be *quite* idle'. He enjoyed himself in Cambridge and his warm, outgoing nature made him many friends, notably Adam Sedgwick, Professor of Geology at Cambridge, and John Henslow, the Professor of Botany. Indeed Darwin's friendship with Henslow grew so close that he became known as 'the man who walks with Henslow'. Both Henslow and Sedgwick encouraged his interest in natural history, and introduced him to the work of the geologists William Paley and Charles Lyell, and the great scientist-explorer Alexander von Humboldt. While still an undergraduate, Darwin gained a reputa-

***Dr Erasmus Darwin***
*Charles' grandfather (top) in his book* Zoonomia *(65 years predating the* Origin*), had asked whether 'all warm-blooded animals have arisen from one living filament?'*

***Brother and sister***
*(above) Charles (aged six) pictured with his younger sister, Catherine.*

Victoria and Albert Museum/Bridgeman Art Library

***Mother and family***
*(above) Seated on horseback is Susannah, with her parents Sarah and Josiah Wedgwood on the right.*

***Country life***
*(below) Darwin's father told his son: 'You care for nothing but shooting, dogs and rat-catching, and you will be a disgrace to yourself and all your family.'*

tion as one of the leading British amateur naturalists.

When he graduated from Cambridge in 1831 Adam Sedgwick took him on a surveying trip in North Wales. On his return to The Mount at the end of August, he found awaiting him an invitation from the navy to join *HMS Beagle* as naturalist on a survey trip around the world. Darwin was only 22 – it was the chance of a lifetime.

## VOYAGE ON THE 'BEAGLE'

His father was at first reluctant to let him go, but was persuaded by Charles' uncle Josiah Wedgwood, a man for whom both father and son had developed an unbounded respect. By the end of the year, Darwin was sailing southwards in the *Beagle*, equipped with all the naturalist's standard gear and a large library that included Charles Lyell's recently published *Principles of Geology* – a classic book that laid the groundwork for Darwin's theories by establishing that the world is much, much older than the Church of the time stated.

The voyage lasted almost five years, and the experience was priceless. As the *Beagle* sailed on round the world, Darwin collected thousands of wonderful speci-

***An abandoned career***
*Charles was expected to become a doctor, following in both his father's and his grandfather's footsteps. But witnessing operations carried out without anaesthetics (left) convinced Darwin that a career in medicine was not for him.*

7

mens and sent them back to Henslow along with detailed explanatory letters. Henslow publicized the contents of these remarkable letters and by the time Darwin arrived back home in October 1836, his name was well known. More importantly, it was the observations made on this trip, especially on the Galapagos Islands, 500 or so miles off the west coast of South America, that were eventually to lead him to his theory of evolution by natural selection.

He returned to England a changed man. Gone was the old frivolity and carelessness. He was now a deeply thoughtful young academic – quite sober-minded enough for his father to provide him with an income which ensured that he would never have to look for a career again.

## NATURAL SELECTION

Immediately he got back, Darwin settled in London to sort out his collection and write up his journal for the voyage. As he worked diligently away, he became more and more convinced that the different species had not been fixed once and for all, as was widely believed, but were continually changing. He was not alone in this belief, but he was alone in his determination to prove it. Established in a flat in Great Marlborough Street, he began by sending out questionnaires to horse breeders, cabbage-growers, zoologists – anyone who could provide him with clues.

Gradually, he began to build up a mountain of evidence in support of the transmutation of species (that is, evolution). He continued to write up his journal of the *Beagle* voyage, but devoted more and more time to the species problem.

By the middle of 1838, he was beginning to show signs of the ill-health that was to dominate his remaining 40 years, and may have been the reason for his reclusive life. Many people in his lifetime accused him of malingering and hypochondria – an accusation he vehemently denied – but he was probably suffering from Chagas' disease, a debilitating tropical illness he caught when bitten by a Pampas bug during the *Beagle* voyage. But his work went on and, early in 1839, the *Beagle* journal was published. It was beautifully written, captivating the non-specialist reader as well as the scientist.

Even before the publication of the *Beagle* journals, Darwin had become a popular figure in London academic circles, sought after by eminent men like the geologist Charles Lyell and the botanist Joseph Hooker. But there was something he disliked about London. He longed for Shropshire and the countryside. He longed for something else, too, and in July he sat in his room carefully weighing up the pros and cons of marriage: 'Imagine living all one's day solitarily in smoky, dirty London – only picture to yourself a nice soft wife on a sofa with good fire, and books and music perhaps . . . Marry – Marry – Marry: Q.E.D.'

He probably knew already who he wanted to marry: Emma Wedgwood, his cousin and childhood friend from Maer Hall. But it took him a long while to pluck up courage to ask, and it was not until November that he finally made his proposal. According to his daughter Henrietta, 'He was far from hopeful, partly because of his looks, for he had the strange idea that his delightful

***Emma Darwin***
*Emma Wedgwood Darwin was Charles' cousin, friend, and then wife. Although sceptical about his ideas on evolution, which challenged her religious beliefs, she nevertheless loved and supported her husband throughout his life.*

***The 'Beagle'***
*The five years Darwin spent on the 'Beagle' were to change his life, and to lead to his theory of evolution. The 'Beagle' docked in Sydney harbour (right) on 12 January 1836, towards the end of its epic round-the-world voyage.*

face, so full of power and sweetness, was repellently plain.' Emma had no such doubts. Nor did her father Josiah Wedgwood, who wept for joy when told. They were married in January 1839.

The marriage was an extremely happy one, and they had ten children all of whom Darwin treasured unreservedly. Emma Darwin never accepted the ultimate implication of Darwin's work – the unreality of the biblical Creation story – but the difference seemed to cause no friction between them, and she was happy to spend her life with him and raise their family.

It was about the time of their marriage that Darwin's belief that species survived by adaptation began to crystallize, and it may have been in the library at Maer Hall that he read Malthus' treatise on population. Malthus' proposal that population growth was self-limiting

***Down House***
*(above) Painted by Darwin's niece, Julia Wedgwood in 1886, Darwin lived here from 1842 until his death over 40 years later. Down House was situated 19 miles from London and formed an ideal base, despite the fact that it had neither bathroom nor running water. It gave him the seclusion he cherished and allowed him to continue his writing and research undisturbed.*

## THE WEDGWOOD CONNECTION

**C**harles Darwin's marriage to his cousin Emma Wedgwood in 1839 saw the continuation of a close bond between two remarkable families that lasted for well over a century. The Wedgwoods were one of the great liberal families of the early Industrial era. Emma's grandfather, Josiah Wedgwood I, is best known for creating the world-famous Wedgwood potteries in Staffordshire, while his youngest son Thomas was the first person successfully to record a camera image.

*This Wedgwood cameo illustrates the family's campaign against slavery.*

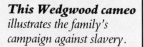

**Josiah Wedgwood II**
*'Uncle Jos' was instrumental in young Charles sailing on the 'Beagle'. He achieved fame by campaigning for the abolition of slavery and in setting up the Royal Horticultural Society at Kew.*

suggested to Darwin the idea of natural checks and balances on the growth of species numbers – checks which meant that those individuals poorly adapted to their environment would not survive to pass on their characteristics to their offspring. Over the next 20 years he was to refine and clarify this idea of natural selection and build up a weight of evidence which he finally published in *The Origin of Species*.

In 1842, Darwin and his wife moved to the large, secluded house in Downe, Kent, that was to be their home for more than 40 years. Down House was a rambling, tranquil place, set in 18 acres of ground, where Darwin could work in peace surrounded by his wife, his children, numerous cats, dogs, squirrels, horses and pigeons. He rarely left Down House, except to make trips back to Shrewsbury, to London's scientific societies, or to take a water cure – for he was frequently unwell – but scientist friends like Hooker and Lyell and Thomas Huxley often came to visit.

For 14 years after he moved to Downe, he continued to build up the evidence for his theories, making a special, exhaustive study of barnacles. But he decided not to make his findings public until the evidence could not be disputed. Then in 1855 came the news that someone else, the botanist Alfred Wallace, was also working on an evolutionary theory. Darwin's friends encouraged him to make his work public soon. Slowly and reluctantly, he started to write his great book, sending a letter to Asa Gray at the Linnaean Society to inform him of his ideas. He was only a fraction of the way through his book when, in June 1858, Wallace wrote him a letter from the Moluccas Islands outlining a theory of evolution by natural selection almost identical to Darwin's own.

Darwin was thunderstruck, admitting to Lyell, 'all my originality . . . will be smashed', and asked what he should do. The outcome was a brilliantly productive

Royal College of Surgeons/Down House

compromise. At Lyell's suggestion, Wallace's paper and Darwin's letter outlining his ideas to Asa Gray were presented together at a meeting of the Linnaean Society in July.

Though the papers attracted surprisingly little attention, Darwin immediately set to work writing an account of his ideas. Originally intended as an 'abstract' – or synopsis – it was soon extended to make an entire book. This book, completed in over a year, was *The Origin of Species.*

## THEORY OF EVOLUTION

The first edition of the *Origin* sold out on the day it was published. It created a furore in academic and religious circles and was soon the talk of middle-class Victorian parlours all over England. Soon every thinker in England was debating the case for or against evolution. In his *The Origin of Species,* Darwin studiously avoided anything more than a hint that Man might be implicated in the evolutionary process. But the hint was enough; people inferred that Darwin was suggesting Man had descended from the apes, and before long, furious debates were raging up and down the land.

Throughout the 1860s, as the evidence in favour of evolution by natural selection began to pile up, Darwin continued to work away quietly on a variety of projects, including a treatise on orchids. Then, in 1868, he decided the time was ripe to include Man in his scheme of things, and began work on his third major book *The Descent of Man.* He argued, 'Man in his arrogance thinks himself a great work worthy the interposition of a deity. More humble & I think truer to consider him created from animals.' By August 1870, the manuscript was at the publishers, and early in the following year, it was published.

As Darwin predicted, the book caused as great a stir as *The Origin of Species.* But Darwin, having presented his carefully measured argument, refused to be drawn into the public affray, and remained at Down House

working – this time on the study of the expression of emotions in man and animals and on the power of movement in plants. But he was getting old now, and frail, and he felt time begin to drag. On one occasion, he is said to have gone into the drawing room saying, 'The clocks go so dreadfully slowly, I have come in here to see if this one gets over the hours any quicker than the study one does.'

On 18 April 1882, he suffered the most severe of a series of heart attacks. Recovering consciousness, he whispered calmly 'I am not in the least afraid to die'. He died the following afternoon and was buried in Westminster Abbey on 26 April. After the funeral, the eulogies flowed and many agreed with Huxley who mourned the loss of Darwin's 'intense and almost passionate honesty by which all his thoughts and actions were irradiated, as by a central fire.'

Royal College of Surgeons/Weidenfeld Archives

# THE GREAT DEBATE

When *The Origin of Species* was published in 1859, most people believed that the Creation was a factual account, and that God really had created Man and every species of animal once and for all in the Garden of Eden (below). The words of the Bible were taken literally. By trying to show that species were not fixed but had evolved gradually from a single source, Darwin plunged into a storm of controversy and started a battle of science versus religion that, even today, is unresolved.

One of the most spectacular clashes was that between Darwin's champions, Thomas Huxley and Joseph Hooker, and his vehement critic, Bishop Wilberforce at a meeting of the British Association in Oxford in 1860. The highpoint of the Debate was when Wilberforce asked Huxley, 'was it through his grandfather or his grandmother that he claimed descent from a monkey?' 'I would rather be the offspring of two apes than be a man afraid to face the truth,' Huxley is believed to have replied.

The then Vice-Admiral Fitz Roy (the captain of the *Beagle*) attended the debate, and tried to denounce his former colleague, but was shouted down by Darwin's supporters, and walked out in bewildered fury. To him, and many others, Darwin's theory was an affront to his most sacred beliefs.

**'Soapy Sam' versus 'Darwin's bulldog'**
*Bishop Samuel Wilberforce, known as 'Soapy Sam' because of his glib eloquence, proclaimed before the Oxford Debate that he was out to 'smash Darwin'. He asked Thomas Huxley (known as 'Darwin's bulldog', below) whether it was through his grandmother or grandfather that he was descended from apes, only to be demolished by Huxley's witty riposte.*

# THE VOYAGE OF THE 'BEAGLE'

**Written when Darwin was an eager young naturalist, this compelling
journal tells the story of a voyage of discovery through continents
and time, with consequences that changed the world.**

Adapted from the diary that Darwin kept throughout *HMS Beagle's* five-year journey around the world, *The Voyage of the Beagle* is one of the most fascinating and detailed travelogues ever written – as well as one of the most exciting scientific works written for popular consumption during the 19th century. The journal is a treasure-house of detail. Side by side with meticulous descriptions of the behaviour of a particular South American beetle, for example, are accounts of nights spent camping on the Argentinian Pampas with the gauchos and days spent riding giant tortoises in the Galapagos Islands. These remote, volcanic islands far out in the Pacific Ocean are the focus of the journal's scientific interest. For it was here that the seeds of Darwin's revolutionary theory of evolution were sown.

Darwin was a young divinity graduate when the opportunity came to join the survey ship as an unpaid naturalist: his friend and mentor Professor Henslow had recommended him to the *Beagle's* Captain Fitz Roy. It was Henslow who suggested that he take with him a copy of Charles Lyell's *Principles of Geology* – advising him that he would find the facts useful, but warning him to ignore the

> *"Every form, every shade, so
> completely surpasses in
> magnificence all that the European
> has ever beheld… The general
> effect… recalled to my mind the
> gayest scenery of the Opera-house"*

theory: that the world was millions of years older than it was thought, and that the Earth was not shaped by Noah's Flood, but by natural forces such as earthquakes, winds and rain. According to Henslow, such theorizing was 'altogether wild'.

The survey ship set sail from Devonport (Plymouth) on 27 December 1831. Its first port of call was at the tropical Cape Verde Islands, off the west coast of Africa. Over-joyed to reach dry land after weeks of seasickness, Darwin began his work of collecting data on plant and animal life, taking samples, examining and preserving them, and despatching examples of flora and fauna back to England. He started his copious notes and, with the aid of Lyell's *Principles*, began to try to make sense of local geology. On observing a "perfectly horizontal white bank in the face of the sea cliff . . . about forty-five feet above the water", he climbed up to examine its structure, and found that it was composed of thousands of sea shells – many of them like the shells he had collected on the beach below. How did this band – which appeared to be the ancient sea bed – come to be at the top of a cliff? He realized that some natural force must have pushed the entire coastline upwards until it stood more than forty feet above sea level. With the help of Lyell and geology, the past was beginning to tell him its own story 'with an almost living tongue'.

The *Beagle* sailed on across a calm Atlantic to reach Brazil in February 1832. Darwin was delighted with this naturalist's paradise, and it was from Rio de Janeiro that he made the first of his inland expeditions. With six others, he

**The 'Beagle's'
Captain**
*During the five-year
voyage of the* Beagle
*(right), Darwin shared
a cabin with the moody
Robert Fitz Roy
(above). Darwin
endured his moroseness
until he 'praised
slavery, which I
abominated'.*

Royal Naval College/Bridgeman Art Library

National Maritime Museum, London

travelled on horseback several hundred miles over hills, through lakelands and forests, meeting estate owners, villagers – and slaves. For the first time, he was exposed to the degradation of negro slaves in Brazil, and the journal makes it clear that he detested slavery.

## A SENSE OF WONDER

Returning from his expedition, Darwin settled in the little village of Botofogo outside Rio for three months, collecting specimens, observing, experimenting, and labelling his samples. The detail of his observations reveals the almost poetic sense of wonder with which he viewed the world. He describes a vampire bat biting a horse's withers, a marching army of ants, the "never-failing foragers . . . burdened with pieces of green leaf, often larger than their own bodies", and the "deadly contest" between a wasp and a spider.

At this time, Darwin still believed in what is called the 'fixity of species' – that is, that species were created exactly as they exist in the present day. But he was alive to the idea that animals can change their habits to take advantage of differences in environment. It is also clear that by now, he accepted Lyell's view that the Earth is millions of years old, not thousands, as supposed by the creationists who took the biblical account of the world's Creation literally.

Leaving Rio in July 1832, the *Beagle* headed south (accompanied by a huge shoal of porpoises) for Montevideo in Uruguay. Captain Fitz Roy spent the next two years sailing up and down the south-east coast of South

Christie's/Bridgeman Art Library

Fotomas

***South America***
*While the* Beagle *surveyed the coast of South America from Brazil (above) down to Tierra del Fuego, and up to Peru, Darwin journeyed inland – riding in the Pampas and climbing the Andes.*

***Jemmy Button***
*On board were three Fuegians – returned to their native land in 1833. Darwin had grown fond of Jemmy Button (far left), and was shocked to find him a "haggard savage" (left) a year later.*

America, surveying the coastline. Arriving at the mouth of the Rio Negro in Patagonia, Darwin "determined to proceed . . . by land" the 500 miles north back through Argentina to Buenos Ayres, where he was to meet up with the ship again.

Apart from continuing his meticulous scientific investigations, he experienced more adventures – in a land torn by revolution and by a bloody 'holy' war between the government-backed gaucho army and the tribal Indians – than he could ever have imagined when he left Plymouth two years before. He travelled with an Englishman and five gauchos. He had first met gauchos – the South American equivalent of 'cowboys' – the previous year in Uruguay: *"their appearance is very striking"*, he had written then, *"they are generally tall and handsome; but with a proud and dissolute expression of countenance. They frequently wear their moustaches, and long black hair curling down their back . . . Their politeness is excessive; they never drink their spirits without expecting you to taste it; but whilst making their exceedingly graceful bow, they seem quite as ready, if occasion offered, to cut your throat."*

## ARGENTINIAN ADVENTURES

As the young Englishman and his gaucho comrades set off across the desert, the first night left a lasting impression: *"The death-like stillness of the plain, the dogs keeping watch, the gipsy-group of Gauchos making their beds round the fire, have left in my mind a strongly-marked picture . . . which will never be forgotten."*

On the Argentinian Pampas, Darwin uncovered signs of the distant past that showed uncanny links with the present – links that were to be one of the cornerstones of his eventual theory of evolution. Along an old dried river bed, he dug up the fossil bones of nine gigantic creatures – all now extinct. It was during the years after returning to England that he recognized that these extinct animals

Weidenfeld Archives

***Crossing the Line***
*In the* Journal, *Darwin concentrates on his researches and adventures on land, and gives little information about life on board ship. But his letters home reveal fascinating details of day-to-day routine and particular events – such as the traditional initiation ritual he was forced to undergo when he first crossed the equator (left): 'This most disagreeable operation consists in having your face rubbed with paint and tar, which forms a lather for a saw which represents the razor, and then being half drowned in a sail filled with sea-water.'*

were related to modern, living animals. And from this realization, came the conclusion that each species on Earth could *not* have been created spontaneously and separately. Modern-day animals were, in effect, modified versions of their ancient ancestors.

Before making its way up the west coast of South America, the *Beagle* called at the southernmost tip – the Tierra del Fuego. Three years previously, Captain Fitz Roy had captured a party of native Fuegians and had bought another for a pearl button. Having indoctrinated them with Christian beliefs and given them the somewhat undignified names of York Minster, Fuegia Basket and Jemmy Button, he was now returning them – along

with a missionary – to the Tierra del Fuego.

Darwin was astonished by this cold, savage, inhospitable land, and by its "barbarian" inhabitants. Despite the bitterly cold weather, the Fuegians wore nothing but body paint and a small cloak of hide. Sometimes they wore nothing at all, despite almost freezing temperatures. Observing them sleeping naked "on the wet ground coiled up like animals" was rather too much for his civilized European sensibilities: *"Viewing such men"*, he writes *"one can hardly believe that they are fellow creatures, and inhabitants of the same world"*.

In September 1835, after a long expedition in Chile, the *Beagle* left the mainland behind, and sailed west for over 500 miles until it

reached the remote Galapagos Islands – tips of huge volcanic craters which emerge, as if from nowhere, in the middle of the Pacific Ocean. It was here that Darwin's interest switched from geology to biology, and here that he began seriously to question his belief in the orthodox story of the Creation.

"The natural history of these islands is eminently curious", he writes, describing the island group as "a little world within itself". Many animals he saw there were found nowhere else on Earth, but what really puzzled Darwin was that they bore a *resemblance* to those found in mainland America, differing from them in details of their physical appearance and their habits. If these creatures had

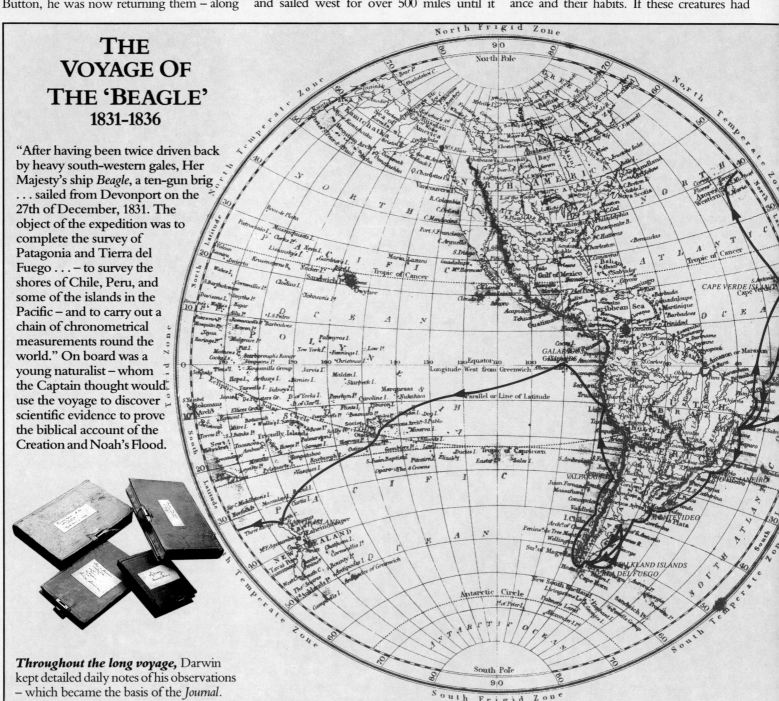

# THE VOYAGE OF THE 'BEAGLE'
## 1831-1836

"After having been twice driven back by heavy south-western gales, Her Majesty's ship *Beagle*, a ten-gun brig ... sailed from Devonport on the 27th of December, 1831. The object of the expedition was to complete the survey of Patagonia and Tierra del Fuego ... – to survey the shores of Chile, Peru, and some of the islands in the Pacific – and to carry out a chain of chronometrical measurements round the world." On board was a young naturalist – whom the Captain thought would use the voyage to discover scientific evidence to prove the biblical account of the Creation and Noah's Flood.

**Throughout the long voyage,** Darwin kept detailed daily notes of his observations – which became the basis of the *Journal*.

been 'created' spontaneously on these far-flung islands, why did they bear a relationship with American creatures separated from them by hundreds of miles of ocean? And why, being so similar, should they differ in details?

He was surprised to find a species of lizard, the iguana, which on the mainland climbed trees and ate leaves, but here lived on rocks and dived for seaweed. He found tortoises, similar to those on the mainland, but these were gigantic specimens, big enough for a person to ride on (which Darwin did). What is more, although these giant tortoises were common to all the islands, their shells differed from island to island.

Darwin was most amazed by the islands "most singular group of finches". Although the 13 species he found were obviously related, they differed in detail, and in particular in the shape and size of beak. The difference was apparently related to the job the beak had to do – whether to crack open hard seeds, or eat soft fruit or insects. *"Seeing this gradation and diversity of structure in one small, intimately related group of birds one might really fancy that from an original paucity [scarcity] of birds in this archipelago [island group], one species has been taken and modified for different ends."* In other words, from one original kind of finch had sprung a family of varied relatives. As yet, Darwin was in the dark about how this could happen. But the data that he accumulated on the "little worlds" with their unique, but related population were to become the basis of his theory of the evolution of species by natural selection.

It would be nearly 25 years before he finally published his theory in *The Origin of Species*. In 1835, his thoughts were turning towards home. From the Galapagos, the *Beagle* travelled on to Tahiti, New Zealand, Australia and finally back to England, arriving in Falmouth on 2 October 1836. Years later, Darwin wrote "The voyage of the *Beagle* has been by far the most important event in my life, and has determined my whole career". In the history of Western thought, it was one of the most important journeys ever made.

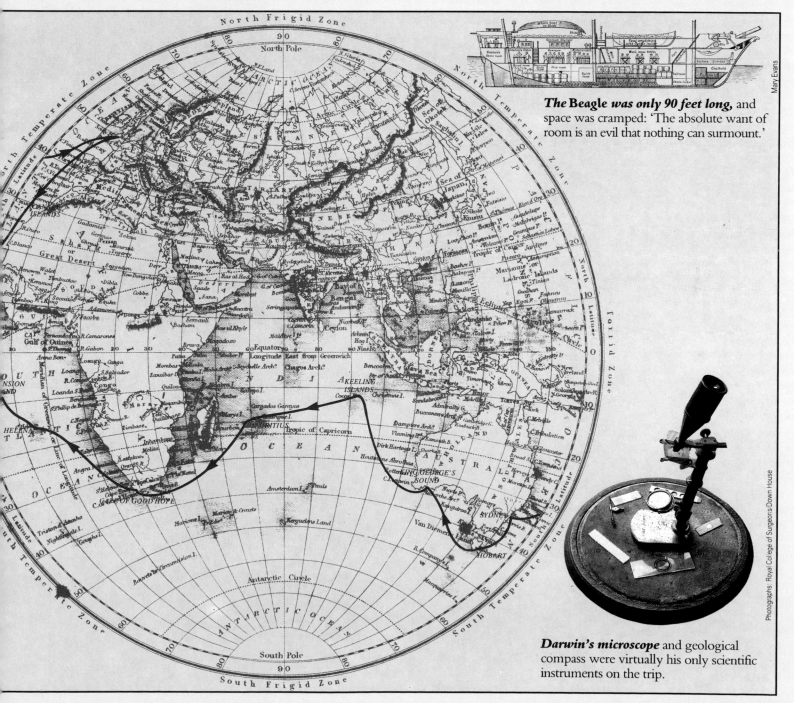

**The Beagle *was only 90 feet long,*** and space was cramped: 'The absolute want of room is an evil that nothing can surmount.'

*Mary Evans*

*Photographs: Royal College of Surgeons/Down House*

**Darwin's microscope** and geological compass were virtually his only scientific instruments on the trip.

# WORKS·IN OUTLINE

Darwin wrote prodigiously on a wide range of subjects: geology, botany, zoology, anthropology, barnacles, coral reefs – even on *The Expression of Emotions in Man and Animals*. But it is his major works on evolution – *The Origin of Species* and *The Descent of Man* – that transformed humans' understanding of themselves and earned Darwin a major and lasting place in the history of thought.

## THE ORIGIN OF SPECIES
#### ✦ 1859 ✦

*On the Origin of Species by Means of Natural Selection, or the Preservation of Favoured Races in the Struggle for Existence* was eventually published after more than 20 years of studying the materials that Darwin had collected during the *Beagle* voyage. He had reached the basis of his conclusion well before 1844, when he wrote to Hooker: 'At last . . . I am almost convinced . . . that species are not (it is like committing murder) immutable [fixed].' Working from three basic facts – that living things vary; that groups of living things tend to increase; and yet the numbers of a species remain relatively constant – Darwin marshalled the evidence to substantiate his theory of evolution: *"As many more individuals of each species are born than can possibly survive; and as, consequently, there is a . . . struggle for existence, it follows that any being, if it vary . . . in a manner profitable to itself . . . will have a better chance of surviving, and thus be naturally selected."* The idea of an unchanging Creation was, he felt, untrue.

### Survival of the fittest
*Darwin's theory was that living beings have become what they are – they evolved from simpler forms of life to fill niches provided by the changing environment. Natural selection means that those animals with variations that are best adapted to their environment – such as giraffes with long necks (above) – are more likely to survive. Those less well adapted will eventually die out (like the archaeopteryx, below).*

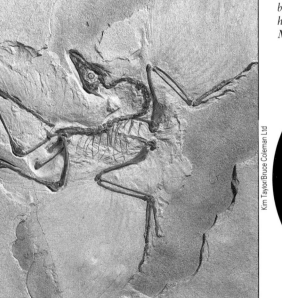

### Two by two or little by little?
*Rather than being the identical descendants of those saved by Noah, Darwin showed that all living beings – from hydra (below) to Man – were the products of evolution. Man-monkey cartoons reflect the common response.*

# THE DESCENT OF MAN
**◆ 1871 ◆**

**In The Origin of Species, *Darwin deliberately avoids including human beings*** in the process of evolution by natural selection – although he does make the understatement: "Much light will be thrown on the origin of man and his history." Most readers saw the implications for themselves, but it was not until *The Descent of Man, and Selection in Relation to Sex* was published, that Darwin finally extended the argument, and made it plausible that instead of descending from Adam and Eve, human beings had evolved from an ape-like primate. Surprisingly, nearly two thirds of the book deals not with human evolution, but with sexual selection – the process whereby some members of a species have an advantage over others by being more attractive to potential mates, and so are more likely to win the 'struggle for reproduction'.

**Beautiful males**
*The second section of* The Descent of Man *deals with sexual selection. An individual is more likely to produce offspring the more attractive he or she is to potential mates. According to Darwin, in most species it is the female who chooses, and the male – like the peacock, "the most splendid of living birds" – who competes.*

J. Savery Noah's Ark (Detail)/Christie's/Bridgeman Art Library

A.J. Mobbs/Bruce Coleman Ltd

Bernarc Gerard/Hutchison Library

Sarah Errington/Hutchison Library

Brian Moser/Hutchison Library

***Darwin noted that human races*** *indicate the variability necessary for evolution. Each race applied its own standards of beauty to sexual selection.*

# UNFAMILIAR FACES

During the voyage of the **Beagle**, Darwin came into contact with many contrasting peoples and societies, and his journal provides a fascinating insight into the responses of a young middle-class Victorian to the native inhabitants and European settlers in distant continents. Coming from an enlightened family, he abhorred slavery – yet he valued "civilized man" more than "savages".

*"I thank God, I shall never again visit a slave country . . .* It makes one's blood boil, yet heart tremble, to think that we Englishmen . . . have been and are so guilty."

*To catch or kill animals on the Pampas* the gauchos used bolas: "the simplest, which is chiefly used for catching ostriches, consists of two round stones, covered with leather, and united by a thin plaited thong, about eight feet long. The other kind differs only in having three balls united by the thongs to a common centre. The gaucho holds the smallest of the three in his hand, and whirls the other two round and round his head; then, taking aim, sends them like chain shot revolving through the air. The balls no sooner strike any object, than, winding round it, they cross each other, and become firmly hitched." When Darwin tried it, the bolas wrapped around the leg of his own horse: "The Gauchos roared with laughter; they cried out that they had seen every sort of animal caught, but had never seen a man caught by himself before."

*The charismatic, ruthless General Rosas* (right) led the gauchos' "villainous, banditti-like army". He was elected to office by being the only man able to jump bareback on a wild horse and bring it into a corral.

Royal College of Surgeons; Down House

Royal Geographical Society

Background illustration: Cathy Morley

Auckland City Art Gallery/Bridgeman Art Library

*Darwin was very critical of the "warlike race"* of the native New Zealanders, or Maoris: "No doubt the extraordinary manner in which tattooing is here practised, gives a disagreeable expression . . . The complicated but symmetrical figures covering the whole face, puzzle and mislead an unaccustomed eye."

*The Australian aborigines,* with their "good-humoured" countenances are described by Darwin as "a set of harmless savages". He admired their skill in tracking and hunting, but could not understand why these hunter-gatherer, nomadic people did not want to settle down, till the ground and tend sheep. He thought that their decreasing numbers were caused by European diseases – he was unaware that they were being systematically murdered by the "civilized" settlers.

André Singer/Hutchison Library

*On seeing the inhabitants of "this savage land",* Tierra del Fuego, Darwin "could not have believed how wide was the difference between savage and civilized man". They went naked in near-freezing temperatures, and Darwin concluded that "nature . . . has fitted the Fuegian to . . . his miserable country". Fuegians probably had a high metabolic rate, which enabled them to survive extreme cold. But they were unable to survive the diseases and cruelty of White settlers – Fuegian Indians are now extinct.

# SPECTACULAR NATURE

Even before leaving England, Darwin was a keen naturalist, but it was not until the voyage of the *Beagle* that he discovered that natural phenomena – past and present – could reveal the history of the world. The variety of environments into which he was plunged, the spectacular geological evidence before him, and his personal experiences of the havoc that could be wrought by Nature led Darwin to believe that the Earth was active and ever-changing – not fixed in a permanent state of perfected Creation.

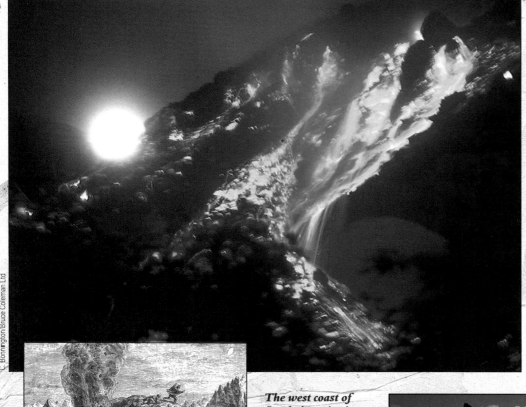

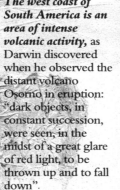

*The west coast of South America is an area of intense volcanic activity,* as Darwin discovered when he observed the distant volcano Osorno in eruption: "dark objects, in constant succession, were seen, in the midst of a great glare of red light, to be thrown up and to fall down".

*"Tremendous and astonishing"* glaciers ran down from the mountainous coast of Tierra del Fuego: "Great masses of ice frequently fall from the icy cliffs, and the crash reverberates like the broadside of a man-of-war, through the lonely channels."

C. Bonnington/Bruce Coleman Ltd

Weidenfeld Archives

Background illustration: Cathy Morley

Jen and Des Bartlett/Bruce Coleman Ltd

*"Among the scenes which are deeply impressed on my mind, none exceed in sublimity the primeval forests* undefaced by the hand of man; whether those of Brazil [left], where the powers of Life are predominant, or those of Tierra del Fuego, where Death and Decay prevail . . . no one can stand in these solitudes unmoved."

*After the lush forests of South America, the Australian deserts* seemed barren; "Clouds of dust were travelling in every direction, and the wind felt as if it had passed over a fire". Darwin left Australia "without sorrow or regret".

*"A bad earthquake at once destroys our oldest associations:* the earth, the very emblem of solidity, has moved beneath our feet like a thin crust over a fluid". During the earthquake that Darwin felt, the Chilean town of Concepcion (above) was razed to the ground.

*Coral reefs and atolls* (right), "these mountains of stone accumulated by the agency of various minute and tender animals!", enthralled Darwin. He wrote the most authoritative book on coral reefs ever written.

*Brazilian flora* (right) delighted Darwin: "The elegance of the grasses, the novelty of the parasitical plants, the beauty of the flowers . . . but above all the general luxuriance of the vegetation, filled me with admiration."

21

# THE GALAPAGOS ISLANDS

*Among the specialized species on the islands* are two kinds of iguana, one of which lives on land (below) in burrows among the scrub: these "ugly animals . . . [with] a singularly stupid appearance . . . try to look very fierce; but . . . they are not so at all; if one just stamps on the ground, down go their tails, and off they shuffle . . ."

- Culpepper I.
- Wenman I.

60 Miles

- Abingdon I.
- Bindloes I.
- Tower I.
- Narborough I.
- James I.
- Indefatigable I.
- Albemarle I.
- Barrington I.
- Chatham
- Charles I.
- Hood's I

Francisco Erize/Bruce Coleman Ltd

Straddling the equator in the middle of the Pacific Ocean, the remote Galapagos Islands are inhabited by unique animals. Their similarities to American species led Darwin towards his theory of evolution. He felt that these species were not the products of an independent Creation, but were the descendants of stranded 'colonists' from the mainland – modified to suit their new environment.

Gunter Zeisler/Bruce Coleman Ltd

*"On the rocky sea-beaches" were "herds" of marine iguana.* "It is a hideous-looking creature, of a dirty black colour, stupid, and sluggish in its movements." Never venturing inland, and eating algae, they do not need to compete with their land-based relatives for space or food.

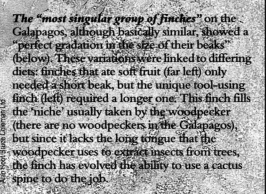

*The "most singular group of finches"* on the Galapagos, although basically similar, showed a "perfect gradation in the size of their beaks" (below). These variations were linked to differing diets: finches that ate soft fruit (far left) only needed a short beak, but the unique tool-using finch (left) required a longer one. This finch fills the 'niche' usually taken by the woodpecker (there are no woodpeckers in the Galapagos), but since it lacks the long tongue that the woodpecker uses to extract insects from trees, the finch has evolved the ability to use a cactus spine to do the job.

1. Geospiza magnirostris.
2. Geospiza fortis.
3. Geospiza parvula.
4. Certhidea olivacea.

*The strangest and most awe-inspiring* of the islands' inhabitants are the giant tortoises – it was their Spanish name, galápago, that gave the islands their name. These "huge reptiles" were "so large that it required six or eight men to lift them". What surprised Darwin was that although the giants were found throughout the archipelago, their shells differed from island to island – as if they had 'diverged' from a common ancestor. As with the other Galapagos animals, these tortoises had no natural enemies until humans arrived. In being an ideal source of fresh meat on long sea voyages, they were pushed to the edge of extinction.

# Natural Delights

**From pond-dipping to eating rhino pie in the bush, ardent Victorian amateur naturalists seemed willing to go to any length in search of new species and new experiences.**

When Darwin was a child scouring the Shropshire countryside for beetles and birds, an interest in natural history was regarded as a little odd. A naturalist was someone who 'went "bug-hunting" simply because he had not the spirit to follow a fox' (although this was hardly true of the young Charles Darwin). But by the time Darwin had finished writing his journal of the *Beagle* voyage in 1838, natural history was well on the way to becoming the most popular of all Victorian pastimes, attracting thousands of ardent enthusiasts up and down the country.

Summer weekends would see many a Victorian gentleman – and some ladies too – donning sensible shoes, picking up a good, stout walking stick and strolling out in the countryside to 'botanize' and observe the wonders of nature. It was not unusual to catch sight of an elderly clergyman bending his arthritic back for a closer look at humble woodspurge or an unfamiliar beetle. Seashores became an especially popular destination for amateur naturalists, possibly due to Philip Gosse, whose exuberant explorations of rockpools and beaches near his Minehead home attracted many an enthusiastic disciple.

## ZOOS AND GARDENS

Observation, though, was rarely enough. To capture the experience, and for the sake of 'science', specimens had to be collected. Wildflowers, fungi and ferns were uprooted from the ground and taken home for examination under the microscope or for display in the study. Butterflies were netted and many an unfortunate bird and wild animal ended up stuffed and mounted in a fine glass and mahogany case. It was a time when naturalists went out armed with a gun, not a camera, and the art of taxidermy was a thriving business. Countless Victorian homes were adorned with natural history specimens, which were as much a feature of some parlours as the displays of expensive porcelain, and tinted prints. Aquaria and ferns were especially popular – although every couple of years a new kind of plant or creature became the focus of attention.

Exotic species excited the Victorian natural historian, and the general public, as much as, if not more than local wildlife. The first half of the century saw zoological and botanical gardens established in towns and cities all over Britain to house and display some of the weird and wonderful specimens brought back from the tropics by intrepid adventurers such as Darwin himself. Of all the gardens, none was more famous than the Royal Botanic Gardens at Kew in Surrey. The original plant

**Botanists botanizing** *(right) were a familiar sight in the lanes, fields and woodlands of Victorian England.*

Marv Evans Picture Library

collection dated from the end of the 17th century, but the real work of establishing the nine-acre plot began in 1759 under the eye of George III. The first official director was Sir William Hooker whose son, Joseph, succeeded him to the post in 1865 and travelled as far as Tibet in search of rare specimens. Joseph Hooker was both a friend and champion of Darwin's. Kew and the new Regent's Park Zoo were kept constantly in the headlines by the *Field* columnist Frank Buckland.

Buckland was a national figure – though with a rather strange penchant, surprisingly common at the

**Margaret Fountaine** *had a strict Victorian upbringing, but broke a great many conventions travelling the world collecting butterflies. Her diaries (above) record as much about her encounters with men as with butterflies: her adventurous spirit did not stop short at lepidoptery. She is pictured right collecting in the United States where she once earned a living gathering spiders' nests at four dollars a dozen.*

Both photographs: Castle Musuem, Norwich/Sunday Times, London

**Alfred Wallace**
*(above) sent Darwin, in 1858, his latest paper to read. The paper reached the selfsame conclusions Darwin had spent 20 painstaking years compiling. "I never saw a more striking coincidence," wrote Darwin. But the 'coincidence' only really indicates the great preoccupation with natural sciences at that time.*

**'glowing accounts'**
*Alexander von Humboldt (above) travelled the equinoctial regions of America between 1799 and 1804. His Personal Narrative of his travels was one of the few books Darwin took on his famous voyage. For Darwin, as for others, Humboldt's narrative fired the imagination and revealed the secrets of Nature: 'he like another Sun illuminates everything I behold'. The compliment was returned – Humboldt read Darwin's accounts of tropical nature with deep interest and was lavish in his praise of Darwin's powers of observation.*

time, for 'zoophagy' (eating wild creatures). Beginning as a schoolboy with squirrel and mice in batter, he graduated to rhino pie (which he cooked before his lecture audiences), giraffe cooked 'on the hoof' (when the giraffe house at the zoo caught fire), panther (already dead and buried three days before he dug it up for the pot), elephant's trunk soup and virtually every British species of wild bird.

### BATS AND BALONEY
Often, the study of natural history became hugely competitive, and it was soon every natural historian's dream to discover a new species, or identify a particularly rare example. Sometimes, species hunting went to quite ridiculous extremes. The famous American bird-illustrator Jean Jacques Audubon claimed that his rival William Swainson 'never goes to bed without describing some new species' – a tendency he and many others were equally prone to.

The eccentric Audubon was once visited by the even more eccentric Constantine Rafinesque-Schmaltz. He woke one night to find his guest running round the house naked, clutching Audubon's valuable Cremona violin and beating it violently against the walls in his attempts to down a bat of a species he claimed to be new. Audubon's revenge for the destruction of his fiddle was to keep slipping into Rafinesque's notes illustrations of invented species, such as the Devil-Jack

Diamond fish which had bullet-proof scales. Rafinesque included these species in his book with the addendum, 'This genus rests altogether on the authority of Mr Audubon who presented me with a drawing of the only species belonging to it.'

### GLOBE-TROTTING BOTANISTS
In their desire to find new species, naturalists would go literally to the ends of the Earth. Darwin, who voyaged round the world in that capacity on the *Beagle,* was just one of the many who journeyed far and wide in the early 19th century in search of new species, either as official naturalists on naval voyages of exploration, or as independent travellers. The German scientist-explorer, Alexander von Humboldt, was by far the most famous, and was much admired by Darwin, but there were numerous others.

South America in particular seemed to draw the intrepid naturalist-explorer like a magnet. Humboldt voyaged up the Orinoco and scaled Chimborazo, then thought to be the highest mountain in the world, while Charles Waterton voyaged up the Essequibo again and again between 1812 and 1825, bringing back numerous birds and animals each time – once wrestling with an alligator to ensure its capture.

In the 1840s, Henry Bates and Alfred Wallace (the naturalist whose theory of natural selection was announced along with Darwin's in 1858) made many dangerous expeditions through the Amazon basin to discover new species. In his 11 years in South America, Bates – who threw up his job as brewery clerk in Buxton to go exploring – collected 14,000 specimens, of which 8,000 were of previously unknown species. Later in the century, women, typically as illustrators, made equally brave voyages, and Marianne North came back with a wealth of beautiful paintings showing the plants she had seen on her trips everywhere from Brazil (1873) to Borneo (1876).

Margaret Fountaine, a clergyman's daughter born in 1862, travelled all over the world in search of butterflies, men and adventure. She voyaged from South Acre near Norwich to Budapest, Turkey, the United States, Africa, India and to the borders of Tibet, dying eventually on the island of Trinidad 78 years later, with a butterfly net at her side. She bequeathed to the world ten handsome mahogany display cases containing no less than 22,000 butterflies, her 'diurnal lepidoptera', and twelve volumes of diaries spanning her life from the age of 15 to a few months before her death. These, she wrote in her will, were not to be opened until 100 years after her first entry, and accordingly we did not discover about the loves and exploits of this extraordinary woman until April 1978.

Some idea of the huge interest in natural history in mid-Victorian England is given by the wealth of literature on the subject. All the daily newspapers had a natural history column. So too

did many of the general interest periodicals. Popular natural history journals like the *Field* had large circulations among the middle classes, while the *Entomologist's Weekly Intelligencer* was bought and read avidly by thousands of working-class men and women every week.

### BEST-SELLERS

But surprisingly it was books which fed most Victorians' fascination for the subject. Natural history books were second only to novels in popularity, and when a Victorian gentleman wandered into the drawing room for a quiet read, he was as likely to pick up something like *The Marvels of Pond Life* as the latest Charles Dickens story. Books on natural history sold in huge numbers and successes like the Reverend J.G. Wood's *Common Objects of the Country* which sold 100,000 copies in a week were by no means unusual.

Forerunners of these books were the perennially popular journals of the 18th-century Hampshire vicar, Gilbert White, and his *Natural History of Selborne* (1789) went through numerous editions in the early Victorian

**What could be more charming**

*and edifying than a family ramble (right), studying the wonders of God's creation? So thought pious Victorians – until Darwin drew their attention to some unfortunate fundamentals in Nature: kill or be killed; only the fittest survive. The romance paled. No longer could quaint human characteristics be attributed to animals: easier to attribute bestial characteristics to people.*

**Edward Lear**

*Though best remembered for his nonsense verses, Lear was primarily a painter of natural studies, such as the Toucan, above left. Collectors commissioned him to immortalise their menageries. Precise, perfect illustrations were vital for systematic classification of plant and animal life. Naming and categorizing were the rage, largely thanks to the Linnaean System (example above) developed in the 18th century by Carolus Linnaeus.*

### A dangerous pursuit

*The aged clergyman strolling through the countryside could furnish only so much information for the new sciences. Some dedicated naturalists exposed themselves to enormous risks in pursuit of knowledge. Charles Waterton, for example climbed treacherously dangerous cliffs to gather birds' nests (right) and even wrestled with an alligator in South America.*

### Lost explorers

*Grisly perils awaited those who went abroad in search of uncharted, unrecorded wonders. But this was the age of the heroic exploit. It took little to justify an expedition of exploration, and the various scientific societies were eager to finance such trips. The Royal Society of Victoria, for example, sponsored the disastrous Great Northern exploration of Australia. Despite the despatch of equally heroic rescue parties (below) all but one of the explorers died.*

period. After reading *Selborne* as a child, Charles Darwin could not understand why every gentleman did not become a naturalist. Dozens more such books appeared, including Darwin's three major works, the *Beagle* journals (1839), *The Origin of Species* (1859) and *The Descent of Man* (1871). Indeed, it seemed that nearly every country vicar and reasonably literate lady (and some not so literate) wanted to write a nature book and kept meticulous diaries to that end.

Many of the authors of the day were well-informed and could back up their claims with considerable experience in the field. Others, however, were more inclined to rely on flowery prose, or anecdotes, which inevitably led to certain myths becoming popular. One famous 'fact' averred in many natural history books was the supposed ability of toads to live forever when encased in rock – at the Great Exhibition of 1862 a toad was on show which was believed to have emerged from a lump of coal. And Mrs Loudon gave the follow-

ing advice in her book the *Entertaining Naturalist:* 'When in danger of being attacked by a Bull, the best course is to stand still, and open an umbrella, or flap a shawl, or something of that kind, in the Bull's face; as with all his fierceness he is a great coward and only pursues those who fly from him.'

## NO CUDDLY ANIMALS

Even the best-informed authors, such as Darwin, could not refrain from using anecdotes to illustrate their work occasionally. Nor could they avoid the equally universal tendency to credit wild creatures and plants with human qualities, emotions and even morals. In her book *The Herb of the Field,* Charlotte M. Yonge describes the polypody moss as 'one of those cheerful, humble things, that seems to have a kindness for what is venerable and excellent, even in decay.' But this sentimental view of Nature was completely overturned by Darwin's *The Origin of Species* and the seemingly brutal idea of the 'survival of the fittest'.

Darwin had been reluctant to publish his findings on natural selection because of the cataclysmic repercussions they were bound to have. They challenged the accepted beliefs about God and Creation – in the late 17th century the Archbishop Ussher had calculated that God's six-day creation of the world and every creature on it began at 9am on 23 October, 4004 BC. And although in Darwin's day this view was beginning to lose ground, his contemporaries were still aeons away from allowing the possibility that the world and all its inhabitants could be in a state of flux, constantly changing and adapting.

But Darwin did eventually reveal his ideas to the public. And the furore that his writing produced was even greater than the gentle naturalist had ever anticipated.

Ironically, his success led to a decline in popularity of natural history for the lay person. Evolutionary theory and the suggestion of the supremacy of Nature over Creation made the study of Nature the province of the specialist scientist rather than the amateur natural historian. Professional biologists and zoologists were taking over, and by the 1880s the familiar collections of butterflies and birds began to gather dust in attics – forgotten symbols of a previous generation's strange and rather quaint obsession.

***Flora and fauna***
*In 1876, Marianne North went to Ceylon. Hence the addition to her collection of 'Foliage and flowers of a Red Cotton Tree (Bombax malabaricum) and a pair of Common Paradise Flycatchers (Terpsiphone paradisi)' (below).*

***Darwin's kindred spirit***
*The extraordinary Marianne North (above) spent 16 years travelling to remote corners of the world alone, painting superb detailed studies of places and plants. A gallery at Kew Gardens, which she herself endowed, houses her work. It attracted the praise of Darwin who became her friend and advisor – it was he who suggested a further expedition to Australia.*

# HERMAN MELVILLE

## *1819–1891*

Farming, banking, teaching and surveying, Melville tried them all.
His trips to sea might have merely amplified the list had he not had a
gift for exploiting his experiences: 'For a whale-ship was my Yale
College and my Harvard' – this self-taught scholar had found his
metier. For his readers he held the key to a thrilling, virtually
undiscovered South-Sea world. But Melville had grander ambitions.
Ultimately he embarked on a voyage, through his imagination to
arrive at his epic creation, *Moby-Dick*.

# Adventure and Obscurity

**At heart an adventurer, Herman Melville spun magical tales about the uncharted worlds and wild seas he had known in his youth. But much of his life was spent quietly, and in a very different world.**

Melville was made by his adventures. The five years he spent at sea as a young man gave him the impetus and the material for his writing, and resulted in the Great American epic, *Moby-Dick*. Paradoxically, the book heralded its author's literary obscurity rather than fame – a fate with which Melville, perhaps more than most, was able to cope. He once scornfully wrote that 'All Fame is patronage', and his refusal to court public opinion ensured his integrity even if it sacrificed his reputation. It also helped ensure that almost nothing is known about the feelings and personality of this intensely private person.

Herman Melville was born on 1 August, 1819, in New York City, virtually on the doorstep of the Atlantic Ocean. His father, Allan Melvill, imported French clothing; his mother, Maria Gansevoort Melvill, was the daughter of a distinguished general – the 'e' was added to the name after his father's death.

Initially, the family was reasonably comfortable with a staff of maids, a cook and a nurse, but the genteel calm was short-lived. A plague scare months after Herman's birth was the first of a series of disasters for the family. The area around Wall Street was sealed off and the family business there was so badly hit that Melville's father had to be bailed out by relatives.

The troubles continued and Melville's early years were marked by recurrent money problems and instability. When Herman was 12 his father caught pneumonia and died the following year. His wife Maria was left with eight children to feed, clothe and educate and was forced to rely on the charity of relations.

The young Melville inherited from his father a love of travel and adventure (his father had made no less than six trips to Europe by the time he was 31, spending two years in Paris on his first voyage). But he also inherited from him a deep-rooted anxiety about money which was to plague Melville throughout his life.

Shortly after his father's death Melville left school to become a clerk in his uncle's bank, and could well have stayed on had it not been caught in the economic crisis of 1835. From then on Melville moved from one unsatisfactory job to another. He worked on a farm, taught and studied surveying. He drifted in this way for seven years, until his cousin Leonard, who had just returned from a four-year whaling trip, fired his enthusiasm to travel. Melville signed on as a 'boy' on the *St Lawrence* packet ship and sailed across the Atlantic to Liverpool on 5 June, 1839.

There he spent six weeks in the toughest parts of the city, with its beggars, urban decay and squalor. These experiences, and the discovery of a dead woman in an alley with a baby at her breast, stripped away some of the romance of travel, and gave Melville a life-long sympathy for the dispossessed.

When he returned home he found his mother's financial position worse than ever. He tried to help by taking a teaching job, but the school closed down soon after so Melville, with a friend, tried his luck in the West. Little is known about this brief period, but he was back in New York six months later, and, like Ishmael in *Moby-Dick*, he decided "having little money in my purse" . . . "to go on a whaling voyage".

## LIFE AT SEA

Melville signed for the *Acushnet*, according to whose records he was aged 21, 5ft 9½in high, with a dark complexion and brown hair. The whaler sailed out of New Bedford, Massachusetts, on 3 January, 1841. The four-year trip was to be the most valuable of his life.

The *Acushnet* sailed down to South America, on to Cape Horn, through the Pacific whaling grounds and

*Herman's parents*
*(below) Allan Melvill and Maria Gansevoort Melvill were painted by Ezra Ames c. 1820, when Herman was just one year old. His father was of Scottish ancestry, and an ill-fated businessman; Maria Gansevoort was of Dutch stock and her father, General Gansevoort, was believed to be one of the wealthiest men in New York at the time. Allan Melvill died when Herman was 12 years old. Little is known of their relationship, but that Herman was close to his mother cannot be doubted: in 1850, he bought a farm in Pittsfield big enough for his mother and sisters to share.*

The Huntington, San Marino, California

Berkshire Athenaeum

arrived, after 18 months, off the Marquesas Islands. Since Melville had by now had enough of life at sea, he jumped ship with his friend Toby Greene. They had meant to stay with the friendly Happar tribe, but ended by accident among a tribe of cannibals. Although this element is stressed in Melville's *Typee*, he was never in any serious danger and seems to have spent his time, according to his different biographers, 'not at all unpleasantly but not at all happily', doing very little work and, if anything, alarmed mainly by his growing boredom in an idyllic island paradise.

The pair stayed among the cannibals for one month before dashing through the surf to escape and join the *Lucy Ann*, which had pulled into the islands to take on not just these two deserters, but the many others who had been hiding from the *Acushnet*.

His new ship sailed for Japan, but diverted to Tahiti when the captain became ill. Fifteen of the crew, including Melville, refused to serve under his extremely unpopular replacement and were put in the stocks 'to the boistrous mirth of the natives'. As soon as the *Lucy Ann* had sailed on, the local commander released the prisoners, freeing Melville to tour the islands which had recently been colonized by the French.

After four weeks of being an 'omoo' or wanderer, Melville joined the whaler *Charles and Henry*. It sailed in November 1842 for the Japanese whaling grounds, but he discharged himself after six months when the boat anchored in Honolulu. It was here that Melville first encountered missionaries, and he was less than impressed. As far as he was concerned, the missionaries

did not bring the islanders enlightenment, merely slavery. One incident he witnessed typified his view of them – a large female missionary in a cart was being hauled up a hill by an old man and a youth. When they momentarily stopped and paused for breath she smacked them over the head and yelled enthusiastically 'Hookee!' (On! On!).

Melville explored the islands at leisure and then made up his mind to return home, signing for the return voyage of the warship *United States*. This turned out to be the grimmest trip of all. On the first day the crew were summoned to watch a flogging – by the end of the journey Melville had seen a total of 163. He headed straight for home when the ship docked in Boston on 3 October, 1844, and soon after started writing about his adventures, backed up by the accounts of other whalers and explorers.

Everyone thought *Typee*, his first novel, a first-rate read, but some of the critics could not believe that anyone would ever choose to live with a tribe of cannibals. Fortunately Toby Greene, his fellow escapee, was able to verify the story.

The year 1847 was probably Melville's best. He continued his South Sea fiction with *Omoo*, and married Elizabeth Shaw, whom he had known since childhood. The two families had always been friendly. Elizabeth's father had been in love with Melville's aunt and had stayed in close touch with the family after her death. Indeed, one biographer speculated that the links were so close that Melville may have felt a subconscious guilt at this almost incestuous liaison.

**Market Street, Albany**
*(above left) The Melvills moved upstate in 1830, when Herman was 11. While working for his uncles here, the writer (above) began to emerge.*

## Key Dates

**1819** born New York

**1839** sails to Liverpool

**1841** sails to the Pacific

**1842** jumps ship. Lives with the Typee tribe

**1843** returns to USA

**1847** marries Elizabeth Shaw

**1850** moves to Pittsfield. Meets Hawthorne

**1851** *Moby-Dick* published

**1866** made Inspector of Customs NY

**1867** son, Malcolm, dies

**1888** begins *Billy Budd*

**1891** dies in New York

### Elizabeth Shaw Melville

*(left) Herman's wife stood by her husband through all the ups and downs of his life, moving from city to farm and back to city again as his needs and finances dictated, and bearing his four children. Eventually she received a small inheritance which allowed Herman to give up his job as Customs Inspector.*

### Mersey harbour

*Liverpool was a busy port in the 19th century. American ships often docked there, both for trade and pleasure cruises. Fast cargo ships could make the New York to Liverpool run in two weeks but the St Lawrence, which Melville sailed on in 1839 and on which he based* Redburn, *took twice that time. Liverpool proved to be a powerful eye-opener for Melville. Its grime, poverty, disease and general squalor were to haunt Melville and awaken in him the need for social reform.*

The couple honeymooned in Canada, and then returned to New York where they bought a house with Melville's brother Allan, inviting their four sisters and mother to join them.

While Melville's home life improved, his writing career plummeted. His third novel *Mardi* veered away from the earlier autobiographical narrative to a more elaborate structure. But few understood let alone enjoyed its tangle of ethics, religion, philosophy and politics. Being published in an expensive three-volume set did not help, and comments by reviewers like 'tedious and unreadable' and 'the reader will probably detest [it] altogether', finished it off.

Poverty and an extra mouth to feed (Melville's first child Malcolm was born in 1849), meant that he quickly had to write another 'pot boiler', as he termed it. So that same year he concentrated on writing *Redburn*, based on his voyage to Liverpool, and *White Jacket*, about his last leg home on the *United States*.

### FURTHER TRAVELS

Both books sold well, but Melville felt that he had exhausted South Sea stories, and needed fresh experiences to write about. He sailed to London, determined this time to keep a journal to record his thoughts.

To keep fit, each morning he climbed the rigging, much to the delight of his fellow passengers, and on one occasion even induced his two travelling companions to join him in the maintop for their morning conversation! Instead of sailing up the Thames, the three asked to be rowed ashore off Deal in Kent, and then walked the 18 miles to Canterbury, from where they headed for the London sights. Melville filled his time with visiting art galleries, theatres, the Lord Mayor's Show, courts, and even attended a public hanging.

He had intended to use this material for a novel about an American in exile in Europe, but his return

### Richard Tobias Greene

*Friend Toby, who sailed with Melville on the* Acushnet *in 1841. Together they decided to jump ship when the* Acushnet *anchored in Nuku Hiva Bay in the Marquesas Islands and inadvertently found themselves among a tribe of cannibals. When Melville incorporated this episode into* Typee *five years later, his readers were thrilled but sceptical. However one of the readers was Toby Greene himself who contacted a Buffalo newspaper and declared to a reporter 'I am the true and veritable "Toby", yet living, and I am happy to testify to the entire accuracy of the work . . .'*

voyage home refreshed his memories of the sea, and his old passions. Soon after, he set about writing his own masterpiece, *Moby-Dick*.

Meanwhile, since the Melville household had become too noisy and overcrowded for him to concentrate on writing, the entire family moved to a 160-acre farm in Pittsfield, Massachusetts. It was an enormous change for Melville and one he loved. He revelled in the beauty of the place, the sunrises and sunsets, and the unfamiliar joys of feeding his horse and cow and planting vegetables for his family. He would rise at 8am, breakfast and then write intensively until 2.30pm. A special pleasure in the evenings was to ride into town on a sleigh with his mother and sisters.

Melville's lifestyle now was much more conducive to writing and he commented that his head was filled with so many ideas that he wished he had 'fifty fast-writing youths' to transcribe them all on to paper. Another benefit of his move was that it allowed him to meet fellow-writer Nathaniel Hawthorne who had recently published *The Scarlet Letter*. Melville was impressed with Hawthorne's tragic sense, in particular his 'power of blackness'. He was to find him the most stimulating man he had ever met, and the two became lifelong friends. All the while *Moby-Dick*, one of the most potent images in American literature, was emerging, acquiring a greater stature and symbolic significance than anything he had ever tackled before.

## THE BIRTH OF AN EPIC

Melville wrote under intense pressure. He knew that this was going to be his masterpiece, and he knew that he desperately needed to make money to support his family. ('Dollars damn me; and the malicious devil is forever in upon me, holding the door ajar.') Just as pressing were the chores and distractions of home life, which, despite his love of the farm, forced him back to New York to finish the book in peace.

## ENCOUNTERING CANNIBALS

In Melville's first novel, *Typee,* he so strongly condemned the work of the missionaries in the South Seas that he brought the wrath of the Christian establishment down upon him. To Melville, the islanders represented an honesty and simplicity much to be admired. He respected the way they reached out for what they wanted, whether it be food, love or laughter, and in many respects the way they lived was as close to an earthly paradise as anything he had ever encountered. But to the Christian missionaries the 'abandoned voluptuousness' of the natives was an abomination and one to be repressed at all costs. To that end the missionaries employed 'kannakipers' (policemen) to patrol the villages at night and 'in the daytime [to hunt] amorous couples in the groves.'

Melville might have thought there was some justice in the fact that the missionary John Williams (right) and all the Scottish immigrants putting ashore on Eromanga in the South Pacific in 1844 were later killed and eaten by the natives.

*Moby-Dick* was published in 1851 to mixed reviews. Sales were initially good, but later criticisms ended its success. Thirty-six years later it had not even sold 4,000 copies. Melville was extremely resilient but he never wrote again with quite the same intensity. His dilemma was not to be resolved – 'What I feel most moved to write, that is banned, it will not pay. Yet, altogether write the other way I cannot. So the product is a final hash.'

His disappointment with his writing and the precariousness of his finances both took their toll on his health. Despondent about his work, Melville asserted to his friend Hawthorne that he had 'pretty much made up his mind to be annihilated'. He carried on writing but he was no longer in the public eye, and from the age of 37 he slipped into literary obscurity. During this period he travelled in Europe and the Middle East. On his return, financial problems forced him to sell the productive half of the farm and to undertake a three-year American lecture tour.

The tour, however, did not turn his finances around and in 1863 Melville sold the rest of the farm. He returned to New York where, three years later, aged 47, he took his first regular job, as District Commissioner of Customs. His work was extremely routine, involving little more than examining ships' cargoes,

*Fact or Fiction*

## THE WHALE'S REVENGE

Melville may never have hunted a whale that was as terrifying as Moby Dick but stories of similar encounters were well known to him. The legendary 'Mocha Dick' was said to have been harpooned 19 times, to have sunk 14 boats and several ships, and to have caused the deaths of more than 30 men.

First-hand, Melville heard the story of Owen Chase who had been Chief Mate on the whaler *Essex* when it was dashed to pieces by a sperm whale in 1820. Apparently a huge whale separated itself from a shoal of sperm whales that was being hunted by the *Essex* and attacked the ship 'with resentment and fury . . . as if fired with revenge for their [its companions'] sufferings.' Within ten minutes of this ferocious attack, the ship sank without a trace.

but it was what he needed. There, down by the port, he was on familiar territory. His health recovered and for the first time in his life he did not have to worry about money.

Melville worked in the Customs for 19 years. His worst moment during this period was undoubtedly the death of his son Malcolm, who had been so obsessed with guns that he always slept with one under his pillow. The morning after a family row, during which his parents had berated him for the late hours he kept, Malcolm was discovered shot through the temple. Nothing specific is known about Melville's reaction.

## A GRADUAL ECLIPSE

Melville continued writing, but with less urgency than before – the tension in his household had always escalated alarmingly whenever he wrote. Yet in the early 1870s, some four years after his son's death, his wife Elizabeth wrote: 'Herman, poor fellow, is in such a frightfully nervous state that I am actually afraid to have anyone here for fear that he will be upset entirely . . .'

In 1885, the ever faithful Elizabeth received a small inheritance which enabled Herman to retire. He made one final sea trip, to Bermuda, after which he began his last novel *Billy Budd*. He lived long enough to complete it, though not to revise or rewrite it. On 28 September 1891 he died of heart failure.

Melville's life had been one of incredible adventure followed by extraordinary calm. But the last years of his life were spent quietly, almost in obscurity.

It had been so long since Melville had been a popular author that the American press virtually ignored his death. One paper even spelt his name incorrectly. But despite his literary failures which led him to lead an extremely private life, revealing little of his personality, he never stopped writing and challenging popular taste. And he did in the end succeed. *Moby-Dick*, his greatest work, was finally acknowledged as a landmark in American fiction, albeit 70 years after its publication and over 30 years after Melville's death.

### Herman Melville's children
*Above, from left to right: Stanwix, Frances, Malcolm and Elizabeth.*

### Life on the farm
'Preparing for Market' *(left) was painted by N. Currier in 1856 and shows a scene very similar in time and feel to Melville's farm in Pittsfield, Massachusetts, where the author lived happily and productively from 1850 to 1863.*

### Nathaniel Hawthorne
*Herman Melville met Hawthorne in the summer of 1850 and the two remained friends throughout their lives. The little that we know of Melville's private self comes from letters written to his elder colleague and mentor. It was to Hawthorne that he dedicated his masterpiece Moby-Dick and it was his opinion that Melville prized above all others.*

35

# MOBY-DICK

**A titanic struggle between an ungodly old man and a monstrous white whale becomes, in Melville's hands, as powerful as myth and as full of suspense as any magic.**

Transcending all its rivals for imagination, ambition and sustained energetic power *Moby-Dick* is the great 19th-century American novel. Within its pages, Melville tells one of the most exciting adventure stories ever written, and narrates his tale in such rich and vigorous language, investing his subject with such grandeur, that *Moby-Dick* can only be compared with the greatest world literature or – more significantly – with the Old Testament of the Holy Bible.

Four words set the tone. "Loomings!", the title of the first chapter, is ominous and obscure. And "Call me Ishmael", the first sentence, reveals that the narrator has chosen the name of the biblical outcast and wanderer. Building on the theme, the jaunty introduction makes clear that this is a book of doom and that its subject is of mythic proportions. The suspense has begun.

## GUIDE TO THE PLOT

One damp, drizzly November, Ishmael "stuffed a shirt or two into my old carpet bag, tucked it under my arm, and started for Cape Horn and the Pacific." His first stop is New Bedford, the Massachusetts whaling port. There he chooses to lodge in the dilapidated Spouter-Inn, and is directed by the landlord, Peter Coffin, to share a "harpooneer's blanket" with a cannibal from the South Seas named Queequeg. The pair soon become fast friends and set off together for Nantucket, to sign up for a three-year whaling voyage.

Queequeg's curious carved idol, Yojo, decrees that Ishmael must choose the ship, and thus it is that while the cannibal devotes a day to religious fasting, Ishmael signs up on the *Pequod*, a grizzled old ship "long seasoned and weather stained in the typhoons and calms of all four oceans". The ship's owners, Peleg and Bildad, sign him up for a three-hundredth share of the profits; and the next day Queequeg's skill with the harpoon earns him a place, and a ninetieth share.

Vague fears of disaster are already glowering. Before the shipmates go aboard, a cracked sailor named Elijah warns them about the *Pequod's* captain, one-legged Ahab, and alludes to a mysterious group of "shadows" who have slipped aboard the ship. But when the *Pequod* leaves Nantucket on Christmas day, Ishmael and Queequeg are on board. "Meanwhile Captain Ahab remained invisibly enshrined within his cabin."

For a few days, Starbuck, the first mate, rules the ship, aided by the second and third mates, Stubb and Flask. Ahab remains out of sight, though his whalebone leg is heard at night, rapping against the planks with every step. But as the *Pequod* nears the Equator on its course towards Cape Horn, Ahab appears

*Poussin: Jonah Thrown Overboard. Reproduced by gracious permission of Her Majesty the Queen*

before the ship's company. Taking a Spanish gold 16-dollar piece, he nails it to the topmast, proclaiming: "Whosoever of ye raises me a white-headed whale with a wrinkled brow and a crooked jaw . . . he shall have this gold ounce, my boys!"

The chase for Moby Dick – the white whale that took off Ahab's leg on a previous journey – has begun in earnest. The crew soon realise that their captain cares nothing for the profits of the voyage, or the shares any of them will earn.

Though the mates are shocked by Ahab's grim mission, the harpooneers are not. When the crazed captain pours grog into the sockets of their weapons, they drink and pledge to carry out his will: " 'Death to Moby Dick! God hunt us all if we do not hunt Moby Dick to his death!' "

Soon afterwards, a sailor at the mast-head sights a whale, and the boats are quickly lowered to chase it. A new secret is revealed: Ahab has brought his own boatmen, led by the harpooneer Fedallah, a wraith-like "dusky phantom", who has been concealed with his four companions in a secret cabin. But when Ahab sees that the whale is not Moby Dick, he leaves the chase to the others, and returns to the *Pequod*. Ahab has no interest in this sperm whale (which escapes), or the one caught by Stubb a few days later, or the right whale that is his next victim. He cares only for

### The Spouter-Inn
*Ishmael's first port of call is New Bedford, where he lodges at Peter Coffin's inn – the Spouter. Such names are ominous, and help create an atmosphere of foreboding. The camaraderie he finds here is aided by the paraphernalia of whaling – the bar is made from a whale's jaw, a painting suggests a whale attacking a ship, the walls are hung with a "heathenish array of clubs and spears" and the clientele are exclusively whalemen.*

*Fotomas*

**Epic myth?**
*Biblical and literary allusions are plentiful, and pointed, in Moby-Dick. High seriousness, myth, legend and history all play a powerful part in an already powerful story of suspense and adventure.*

**Signing up**
*(below) Queequeg's idol Yojo decrees that Ishmael must choose their ship, and he duly picks the* Pequod – *"A cannibal of a craft, tricking herself forth in the chased bones of the enemies." The owners are "fighting Quakers . . . with a vengeance". After signing up, Ishmael and Queequeg are warned of their doom by a cracked old beggar called Elijah.*

Moby Dick; and as the *Pequod* crosses the South Atlantic and the Indian Ocean, meeting other ships – the *Albatross*, the *Jeroboam*, the *Virgin*, the *Rosebud* – he pauses only to enquire if the white whale has been sighted. When the answer is negative, he sails on at once.

> "Ship and boat diverged; the cold, damp night breeze blew between; a screaming gull flew overhead; the two hulls wildly rolled . . . (we) blindly plunged like fate into the lone Atlantic."

Then they meet the *Samuel Enderby*, whose captain has also fallen foul of Moby Dick – he directs them north past Taiwan towards Japan. Ahab's thirst for vengeance is fired beyond all restraint, and a sequence of bad omens casts gloom over the crew. First the feverish Queequeg has a premonition of death, and orders the ship's carpenter to build him a coffin. Then Ahab hurls his quadrant into the sea, cursing its incapacity to guide him to the whale. Lightning strikes the ship, causing the masts to glow like candles, and ruining the compass. The log and line, which measures the *Pequod's* speed, break during the storm. And at last, with the ship's company utterly dependent on Ahab's seamanship,

comes the cry from the mast-head: " 'There she blows! – there she blows! A hump like a snow hill! It is Moby Dick!' "

The boats are launched immediately, and with Ahab at the fore they chase their terrible prey. For two days they hunt him, and each day the harpooneers plunge their weapons into his flesh. But the whale is too cunning to be caught. He twists, turns and dives, stoving

in Ahab's boat and dragging Fedallah to his death.

On the third day of the hunt, the boatmen see Moby Dick turn from their frail, battered craft to face the *Pequod*. "Retribution, swift vengeance, eternal malice were in his whole aspect, and spite of all that mortal men could do, the solid white buttress of his forehead smote the ship's starboard bow . . ."

As the *Pequod* sinks, with the loss of all hands, Moby Dick surges towards his tormentor. Ahab stands in his boat, cursing the whale: " 'To the last I grapple with thee; from hell's heart I stab at thee; for hate's sake I spit my last breath on thee . . . *Thus*, I give up the spear!' " Only Ishmael escapes the maelstrom.

## MASTERPIECE OF SUSPENSE

The outline of the plot does scant justice to *Moby-Dick*. Melville's masterpiece contains far more than the adventure story, which takes up less than half the book's 135 chapters. The remainder provides a comprehensive, almost encyclopedic account of whales, whaling and the whaling industry.

Such passages may seem uninviting to modern readers, and many have discovered that it is perfectly possible to read and enjoy *Moby-Dick*, skipping the whaling details entirely. But the cost of such personal editing is more severe than appears at first sight; for the essence of *Moby-Dick* is suspense. And the essence of suspense is the author's ability first to arouse in the reader the desire to know what will happen, and then to delay that knowledge until the tension is almost unbearable. Thus the whaling chapters delay the final chase and heighten the excitement when it occurs. By deepening the reader's knowl-

edge of the whale species, moreover, they have the paradoxical effect of making Moby Dick himself grander, more mysterious and more mythical than his kin.

While other whales can be caught, dissected and analyzed, he swims alone, rarely seen, feared even by harpooneers for his size and ferocity, and distinguished from all other whales by the white of his skin. In his chapter *The Whiteness of the Whale*, Melville contemplates the strange hold this colourlessness has on the human imagination, and moves from science into symbolism, urging that white "is at once the most meaning symbol of spiritual things, nay, the very veil of the Christian's Deity; and yet . . . the intensifying

> "...two long crooked rows of white, glistening teeth, floating up from the undiscoverable bottom. It was Moby Dick's open mouth and scrolled jaw... like an open-doored marble tomb..."

agent in things the most appalling to mankind." In passages like this, Melville builds up the significance of his story like a theologian discussing the Bible. Even before he has told the full tale, he is discussing its meaning, and why it should be so powerful. But all the while he is whetting the reader's appetite to know what will happen.

In the main plot, Melville draws on more familiar devices to heighten suspense. Numerous biblical names - Ishmael, the mad sailor prophets Elijah and Gabriel, the ship *Rachel* - bring an atmosphere of religious intensity; and Ahab's own name, we learn, was that of a biblical king: "And a very vile one.

---

*In the Background*

## THE PRICE OF DISOBEDIENCE

**C**aptains of whaling ships held absolute authority over their crew, and disobedience was rigorously suppressed by punishments ranging from fatigue duties to solitary confinement and occasionally to flogging. Starbuck's failure to challenge Ahab is only partly due to Ahab's powerful character – sea law plays an equal part.

***Law of the sea***
*Life at sea was so tough and dangerous that mutiny was common. Floggings were the price of failure.*

***Cutting in***
*Descriptions of the whaling industry add to the suspense of the adventure and heighten its impact. Episodes may be stark and simple – "Now as the blubber envelopes the whale precisely as the rind does an orange, so it is stripped off from the body precisely as an orange is sometimes stripped by spiralizing it." – or they may be drawn from folklore, myth and legend. All serve to make Moby Dick more ominous and foreboding.*

**Majesty of might**
*The Pequod's crew finally meet with Moby Dick and, for three days, are embroiled in a ferocious hunt to the death. Previous chases of ordinary sperm whales (left) cannot compare to the fury of the actions and events, or to the unbridled might of the white whale.*

When that wicked king was slain, the dogs, did they not lick his blood?" Such implied predictions and other premonitions of disaster build the reader's anticipation to fever pitch. And in the figure of Ahab, growing ever more possessed by his mania for revenge on a mythical beast, Melville creates a character so bold and extravagant that his brooding presence dominates even the whaling sections of the book. Slowly but unremittingly Melville

builds the combat between Ahab and Moby Dick into a struggle so heavy with symbolism that critics have read into it any number of different meanings.

### GOOD AND EVIL
Running throughout the novel is one major theme: the struggle between good and evil, symbolized by the colours white and black. But Melville sees no simple patterns here. When Ishmael meets Queequeg, he instantly assumes that this black tattooed cannibal is evil: "I confess I was now as much afraid of him as if it was the devil himself who had thus broken into my room at the dead of night." But he soon finds Queequeg a man of rare nobility and pagan gentility.

Ishmael finds a similar contradiction in the behaviour of the Christians themselves. When he signs up on the *Pequod*, he meets the ship's owners, Bildad and Peleg, who are white men dressed in black: "fighting Quakers; they are Quakers with a vengeance." Bildad sits below deck, reading his Bible, and uses its wisdom to justify his stinginess. Ishmael soon draws the conclusion that virtue is not easily found in human society.

Once on board the *Pequod*, however, the focus shifts from human relationships to that between humans and Nature. Ahab, the ship's captain, is the leader of a closed society, drawn from every corner of the Earth –

Americans, Polynesians, Indians, Chileans: a microcosm of 19th-century America. The ship, a "joint stock company" involved in one of America's most vital industries – the oil business of the time – is nominally a democratic concern, set up to assure profits for all its members. But in practice, it becomes a vehicle for Ahab's demoniac urge.

"*All that most maddens and torments; all that stirs up the lees of things; all truth with malice in it; all that cracks the sinews and cakes the brain; all the subtle demonisms of life and thought; all evil, to crazy Ahab, were visibly personified and made practically assailable in Moby Dick. He piled upon the whale's white hump the sum of all the general rage and hate felt by his whole race from Adam down; and then, as if his chest had been a mortar, he burst his heart's hot shell upon it.*"

As the plot advances, Melville shows Ahab, not Moby Dick, as the embodiment of evil. Starbuck struggles with his moral duty to shoot the captain, or at least chain him; but Ahab's obsession is a far more potent force than Starbuck's "unaided virtue".

But at the climax of the novel, all moral and symbolic overtones are stripped away. Ahab, standing in his battered boat, watching the *Pequod* sink and awaiting Moby Dick's last assault, is no longer a demon, but an old man, wild and pathetic. And when hunter and hunted disappear below the waves, the combat is finally resolved.

# CHARACTERS IN FOCUS

*Moby-Dick* has a varied cast of human heroes, from the towering figure of the demoniacal Ahab, to Pip, his bright little cabin boy. Each has his moment of glory in this conflict between Good and Evil. Using a style close to caricature, Melville gives all his characters strong, distinctive features, which make each of them as unforgettable as the looming spectre of Moby Dick himself.

## WHO'S WHO

**Ishmael** A disenchanted merchant seaman who signs up for the whaling voyage to see the world – and the only crew member to live to tell the tale.

**Captain Ahab** The "supreme lord and master" of the *Pequod*. A "grand, ungodly, god-like man", who lost a leg hunting the white whale and leads his crew on the doomed voyage of revenge.

**Bildad** Part-owner of the *Pequod*. A miserly Quaker, he spends his days studying the Bible, and resents every dollar paid to the ship's crew.

**Fedallah** A Parsee harpooneer and prophet. Smuggled aboard by Ahab to man the Captain's own boat, to the *Pequod's* crew he is "the devil in disguise".

**Queequeg** A fearsomely tattooed cannibal from the South Seas. Matchlessly courageous, he also has a heart of gold and a self-assured tolerance of others. After befriending Ishmael, he becomes Starbuck's harpooneer.

**Starbuck** First mate of the *Pequod*. "A long earnest man", he pleads with Ahab to abandon his fateful mission, but dares not otherwise restrain him.

**Stubb** Second mate of the *Pequod*. "A happy-go-lucky" and brave, tough whaleman, never seen without his small black pipe.

**Pip** The young black cabin boy. Tender-hearted, tambourine-playing, bright and jolly, he "loses himself" by falling overboard. He becomes Ahab's personal attendant – and plays court jester to Ahab's monomaniacal obsession.

Courtesy of The Rockwell Kent Legacies

**"Dismasted off Japan"** by Moby Dick, one-legged Captain Ahab stumps restlessly around the decks on his "barbaric white leg" of whalebone, making a loud and ominous tapping as he does so. Like the *Pequod* itself, Ahab's figure is part-composed of the whales he has spent his life hunting – but his mind is obsessed by only one. "He looked like a man cut away from the stake, when the fire has overrunningly wasted all the limbs without consuming them . . . his whole high, broad form seemed made of solid bronze . . ." The ship's crew are overawed by Ahab and his madness, and are incapable of bending him from his iron will; "moody stricken Ahab stood before them with a crucifixion in his face; in all the nameless regal overbearing dignity of some mighty woe". Blind courage and determination make him more than human and his captaincy is impossible to question – "at times his hate seemed almost theirs".

**"Islanders seem to make the best whalemen",** but the *Pequod* has a crew of 30 men gathered from the far corners of the world. Ishmael, Ahab and the three mates are all American, but the rest come from as far afield as the Azores or the Isle of Man. Their roles are diverse, and though their part in the adventure is small, they comment on the action, like a chorus in a Greek tragedy.

Peter Newark's Western Americana

Andrew Shearbon: Home From Sea (detail)/Fine Art Photographic Library

**"Call me Ishmael"** says the open-natured but discontented narrator. He takes to whaling as "my substitute for pistol and ball", but finds himself increasingly intrigued by its scope, myth and danger. He quickly develops a close relationship, "like man and wife", with the cannibal Queequeg, but his fate is to record a terrible tragedy.

**First mate Starbuck** (in the bows, below) declares "I will have no man in my boat . . . who is not afraid of a whale". Though he pleads with Ahab to give up his diabolical pursuit of Moby Dick, and even contemplates his murder, he concedes; "My soul is more than matched: she's overmanned; and by a madman!"

Mary Evans Picture Library

Mary Evans Picture Library

**"A man can be honest in any kind of skin"**, *and Queequeg's* ornately tattooed body conceals an "essentially polite", dignified and extraordinarily courageous person. Son of a high chief on the island of Kokovoko, he stowed away on a whaler "to learn . . . the arts necessary to make his people still happier than they were" but has become convinced that "even Christians could be both miserable and wretched". Before meeting Ishmael at the Spouter-Inn, Queequeg had been out selling embalmed human heads, but he soon displays his religious fervour by going into a trance over his "little hunchbacked image" Yojo.

*Alabama cabin boy Pip* (right) is a solitary, puny, bright little lad, who entertains the crew with his tambourine. Forced to row in Stubb's boat, he jumps out at a dangerous moment and is left to drown. Though saved, the fear of solitude and death turns him into a prophetic idiot. "He saw God's foot up on the treadle of the loom; and therefore his shipmates called him mad." In touching Ahab's "inmost centre" the two become united – "One daft with strength, the other daft with weakness."

Roy Miles Fine Paintings/Bridgeman Art Library

Benjamin West: Death on the Pale Horse, Philadelphia Museum of Art

# AN EPIC AMBITION

**Melville achieved fame early and with comparative ease. But his determination to write books on a grand, mythic scale was to cost him both fame and fortune.**

Herman Melville began his literary career as a best-selling author, and then made himself into a far greater, but far less popular writer. Instead of conquering his public gradually, as many writers have had to do, Melville won over his readers immediately, only to alienate them because 'a certain something unmanageable' in his make-up drove him on. The neglect of his later work meant failure of a sort during his lifetime. But it also indicated a genius and integrity that led to the triumphant 20th-century resurrection of his reputation. As the mature Melville wrote, with prophetic insight, 'Failure is the true test of genius'.

The young Melville, anxious to earn some money and make a name for himself, proceeded in a very different spirit. He was the first writer to use the South Seas as literary material, and although *Typee* and *Omoo* were based on his own experiences, they were consciously angled to exploit the public appetite for sensation.

In *Typee* and his other autobiographical stories, Melville involved the reader directly by writing in the first person. But although the element of authentic experience was strong, he also used the novelist's licence to describe his involvement in dramatic events at which he was not present. He likewise made careful use of works of reference in order to include the 'travel information' which 19th-

century readers demanded, and to provide vivid touches of detail.

Publication in Britain tended to improve a book's prospects in the USA, so Melville was delighted when the English publisher John Murray included *Typee* in his Home and Colonial Library series. A degree of controversy also helped to improve the book's sales on both sides of the Atlantic, where some readers were scandalized by Melville's descriptions of the Marquesans' sexual freedom, and by his unflattering picture of white missionary influence. However, later in the year of its publication (1846), a second American edition of *Typee* was called for, and Melville obligingly expurgated the text.

The success of *Typee* and its sequel, *Omoo*, enabled Melville to settle in New York, where he made friends among the city's literary figures and plunged into an extensive

London Library

British Library

***Melville's journals***
*(left) of his later travels
provided him with
lecture material.*

**Knickerbocker,**

NEW-YORK MONTHLY MAGAZINE.

VOL. XIII.

NEW-YORK:
CLARK AND EDSON, PROPRIETORS.
1859.

***A source for Moby Dick***
*(above) The study of the
legendary white whale Mocha
Dick – published in the*
Knickerbocker Magazine –
*inspired both the name and the
nature of Melville's own great
whale.*

***Rural tranquillity***
*(left) Melville's farm in
Massachusetts gave him the
peace he needed for his work.*

course of reading. Both had the effect of increasing his literary ambition. Reading in particular stimulated and excited Melville at least as much as his seafaring experiences had done. In fact, very few authors have been so deeply and immediately influenced by other writers' thoughts and images – from Ben Jonson and Shakespeare to *Confessions of an English Opium-Eater*. Literature also influenced Melville's style, as he sought modes of expression other than the strictly realistic.

When he failed to assimilate his sources, Melville's work could be tortuous, and even incomprehensible. These failings are apparent in Melville's third book, the fantastic romance *Mardi*. It was Melville's first work of pure fiction, and he himself emphasized that it was a new departure. He told John Murray that he had begun to experience an 'incurable distaste' for factual narrative, longed to spread his wings for flight, 'and felt irked, cramped and fettered by plodding along with dull commonplaces'.

## SATISFYING THE PUBLIC

The feeling was to remain, despite the critical and commercial failure of *Mardi*. But with a young family to support, Melville buckled down to give the public what it expected of him – absorbing, lightly fictionalized tales of seafaring and travel. In later life he always dismissed *Redburn* and *White-Jacket* with disgust, as 'trash', but this was less a comment on the quality of the books, than on Melville's frustrated literary ambitions. Even more important, perhaps, was the fact that they were written in unforgettably unpleasant conditions – in four months of continuous daily sessions, in the heat of the summer. To add to Melville's feeling of being enslaved and restricted, a cholera epidemic made it unsafe to venture into the streets of New York.

For many readers, *Redburn* and *White-Jacket* marked Melville's return to his true vein, but

Courtesy Berkshire County Historical Society

although the *Literary World's* objections to Melville's supposed violations of 'the most sacred associations of life' struck an ominous note. The biblical atmosphere of *Moby-Dick,* and the titanic struggle in which Ahab and the white whale are opposed as forces of good and evil, struck many of Melville's critics as perilously close to blasphemy. Although Hawthorne praised *Moby-Dick,* and Longfellow found it 'very wild, strange and interesting', the book pleased few ordinary readers, and it proved a commercial failure.

Melville remained optimistic, though his view of the literary market-place was becoming less than realistic. His next novel, *Pierre or The Ambiguities* would not be 'a bowl of salt water', he declared, but 'a rural bowl of milk'. But his English publisher, Richard Bentley, refused it, seeing that Melville's patchily brilliant investigation of youthful idealism would fail. He was right – the American edition of *Pierre* was a disaster, selling less than 300 copies.

## MAGAZINE FICTION

Temporarily 'blocked' and out of favour as a novelist, Melville started to write for magazines. *Putnam's* took his first story, *Bartleby,* paying him the high rate of five dollars a page. And for three years he found American readers surprisingly receptive to stories that were often more or less parables. But real enthusiasm was reserved for the Melville of *Typee* and *Omoo*, and a series of sketches about the Galapagos Islands, *The Encantadas,* was hailed by the literary critic of *The New York Evening Post* as a welcome come-back after 'such distempered dreams as *Mardi,* and frightful nightmares like the ambiguous *Pierre.*'

It was during this period that Melville for the first time published a novel as a magazine serial. In *Israel Potter,* he had to adapt himself to the demands of the serial form, dividing his narrative into nine roughly equal and self-contained parts. The story – a historical novel – was intended to be magazine fiction, and Melville promised that there would be 'very little reflective writing' in it. He probably managed to maintain a certain emotional distance, although there is arguably a subjective edge to his summary of Potter's life as 'One brief career of adventurous wanderings, and then forty torrid years of pauperism.'

The failure of *The Confidence Man* (1857) ended Melville's literary career, in the sense that he no longer tried to make a living by writing. His need to produce, even while employed in the Customhouse, was satisfied by the verse he wrote on quarter-sheets of paper, cut to size so that they fitted into his pocket. His major effort *Clarel* (1876) was, as he grimly predicted, 'eminently adapted for unpopularity'.

***Images of power***
*Melville was not alone in wishing to depict subjects of a grand mythical nature. In art, painters such as Benjamin West had already explored sublime and heroic themes (above). But Melville's public was never able to make the imaginative adjustment necessary to appreciate the epic quality of his writing.*

***A critic's view***
*(right) The poet Walt Whitman contributed to the success of* Typee *and* Omoo *with his favourable reviews in a Brooklyn magazine. His pronouncement on* Typee *was 'a strange, graceful and most readable book'.*

even when toiling away on them Melville had told his father-in-law of his 'earnest desire to write those sort of books which are said to "fail"'. And, by 1850, the 'certain something unmanageable' took over. He had almost completed a story about a whaling voyage, but continued to wrestle with it, making it more complex and profound.

This was partly the result of Melville's fruitful contact with another writer, Nathaniel Hawthorne, and partly his own discontent with what he could do so well. ('Think of it!

To go down to posterity . . . as a man who lived among cannibals!') But the main impulse came from his own late but swift inner development, which he described in a famous letter to Hawthorne. Employing the image of a flower-like unfolding, he rightly asserted that 'I am now come to the inmost leaf of the bulb'. And in October 1851, instead of the planned 'agreeable narrative', the wild, majestic *Moby-Dick* was published.

By no means all the early reviews of Melville's masterpiece were unfavourable,

## The Writer at Work

Ironically, the work now closest to *Moby-Dick* in fame lay undiscovered for years. Melville finished *Billy Budd* shortly before his death and it was later packed tidily away by his widow. So this compelling tale of innocence and evil set at sea remained unknown, until the revival of interest in Melville prompted its publication in 1924.

With the extraordinary exception of *Billy Budd*, all Melville's fiction was produced before he reached the age of 37. His virtues and faults – those of a self-educated, passionate reading man – were emphasized by his willingness to take risks. He mastered a range of styles from high rhetoric to spare realistic prose, and his range of themes was astonishingly wide and ambitious. They include the great moral and intellectual conflicts – between good and evil, providence and free will, faith and reason, social obligation and moral integrity.

In Melville's best work, his great universal themes are not superimposed on the narrative, but arise naturally out of it. They reverberate through the characters and events, indefinite and suggestive, susceptible to a variety of interpretations. They are like the ancient myths that haunt the world's imagination; and it is as the maker of towering modern myths that Melville stakes his most important claim to greatness.

### Colourful images
*Melville's bizarre and exotic experiences in the South Seas gave his early books their 'stranger than fiction' appeal. His truthful rendering of the islanders' sexual freedom fascinated as well as scandalized the 'civilized' world, and helped not a little towards making his name.*

### Writing in obscurity
*(below) With his later loss of popularity, Melville was forced to take a job as a customs official in New York Harbour. Yet he continued to write in earnest, composing poetry in between his daily inspections of ships' cargoes.*

Melville is one of the great writers of the sea, with an unrivalled command of atmospheric description and a superlative gift as a teller of tales. Most of his books can be enjoyed simply as exciting narratives of travel and adventure, but Melville also strove increasingly to introduce new dimensions of meaning into his material. *Typee* and *Omoo*, his earliest works, for all their enchanting pictures of South Sea island adventure, are also meditations on the dubious advantages of 'civilization' over 'savagery'. In *Mardi*, Melville experimented audaciously with fantasy and philosophical romance. *Redburn* and *White-Jacket* contain, among other things, devastating indictments of conditions on board ship. And *Israel Potter* demonstrates Melville's ability to enter imaginatively into his country's past.

At the end of his life, after years of neglect and obscurity, Melville repeated the symbolic feat he had achieved with *Moby-Dick* by writing *Billy Budd*, a work of genius that did not come to light until after his death, and was published only in the 20th century.

## OMOO
### ✦ 1847 ✦

(below) *'A Narrative of Adventures in the South Seas'* is the subtitle of Melville's second book *Omoo* (the wanderer), which continues the story of Tom (Melville), after his escape from the Typees. Rescued by the ship the *Julia*, he signs on, to find that the conditions on board are appalling. When the mutinous crew (including Tom) bring the ship into Tahiti, and refuse to leave, they are imprisoned for a time. Tom and his seaman friend Dr Long Ghost scrounge a living working on a potato plantation and beachcombing, until Tom decides to leave the island and join a whaling ship. On one level an exciting adventure story, *Omoo* also gives a lively, and often grotesquely satirical picture of the degrading effect of the White man on island culture.

The Whaling Museum, New Bedford

## TYPEE
### ✦ 1846 ✦

(above) *The beautiful Polynesian Marquesas islands* are the setting of Melville's first book, subtitled 'A Peep at Polynesian Life'. Originally published as non-fiction – the events are closely linked to the adventures that Melville himself experienced in the South Seas in 1842 – it tells the story of two seafaring men, Tom (the narrator) and Toby. Tired of their hard life on a whaler, the two friends jump ship and escape to one of the Marquesas islands. After braving precipices and cataracts, they enter into the peaceful valley where the Typee tribe lives. The Typees are reputed to be cannibals, but seem friendly, and allow Toby to leave in order to find help for his injured companion Tom. When Toby is shanghaied onto an America-bound ship, Tom is left alone with the tribe. He enjoys his semi-captive, yet idyllic life with a native girl Fayaway, although he is uneasy about the idleness of his existence. But when the tribe insists that he be tattooed like them, he starts to fear that they have plans to eat him, and makes a difficult escape – finally being saved by the Australian ship the *Julia*. Despite the controversy caused by its scathing attacks on missionary and White imperialist influence, *Typee* was among Melville's most popular books during his lifetime. Reservations about the authenticity of the account were stilled when 'Toby' (Richard Tobias Greene), whom Melville believed dead, reappeared and confirmed its truthfulness.

E.G. Isabey: Boat in a Storm/City of York Art Gallery/Bridgeman Art Library

## MARDI

### ✦ 1849 ✦

*(right) The sighting of a Polynesian boat* containing a native priest, his sons and a White woman intended for sacrifice draws the sailor Taji into a strange tale of mystery, violence and love. Events take him on a symbolic journey around the globe. Taji, a deserter from a whaling ship, determines to save the woman, Yillah. He kills the priest, and sails for the paradise island of Mardi, where he is received as a demi-god. He and Yillah live blissfully together, until Yillah is carried off by the dead priest's sons. Taji and four Mardian companions – a king, a poet, a historian, and a philosopher – set out to search the world for her. Their search takes them to Dominora and Vivenza (thinly disguised satirical portraits of Great Britain and the United States), and to Serenia, where Alma (Jesus) rules with a doctrine of love – which his subjects ignore. When Taji discovers that Yillah has already been sacrificed, he continues his quest alone 'over an endless sea', pursued by the priest's sons. This allegorical romance was Melville's first work of pure fiction. Not surprisingly, contemporary readers found its meandering narrative and heavily loaded symbolism impossible to follow.

National Maritime Museum, London

## BILLY BUDD

### ✦ 1891 ✦

*The handsome, innocent young sailor, Billy Budd* (left) is the hero of Melville's most important work after *Moby-Dick*. Billy is partly modelled on Jack Chase, the English captain of the maintop on board the *United States* when Melville sailed on her. The action (based on a real shipboard court martial) takes place on a British warship in 1798, when Britain was at war with revolutionary France. Billy, a pressed man – " 'Apollo with his portmanteau' " – soon wins the love and admiration of his shipmates, with one exception. The master-at-arms, John Claggart, nurtures an insane hatred for him, and accuses Billy of instigating a mutinous plot. Appalled by this slander, Billy, who suffers a crippling stammer at moments of extreme stress, is unable to answer. Instead he strikes Claggart on the temple and kills him. At this the Captain exclaims, " 'Struck dead by an angel of God! Yet the angel must hang!' " Billy is court-martialled and convicted, yet he seems untouched by his fate. As he is hanged, he shouts, " 'God bless Captain Vere!' ", and in death he appears a Christ-like figure, bathed in an aura of sunlight. The sailors see that a chip of the spar from which he was hanged "was as a fragment of the Cross". The book closes with a moving poem as an epilogue. The finished, but unrevised manuscript of *Billy Budd* was found in Melville's desk after his death. It was overlooked until the revival of interest in Melville's work in the 1920s brought about its belated publication. *Billy Budd* has now also achieved wide fame as an opera by the English composer Benjamin Britten.

National Maritime Museum, London

## REDBURN/WHITE JACKET

◆ 1849/50 ◆

**The rakish English aristocrat Harry Bolton** (right) is just one of the colourful characters encountered by ship's-boy Wellingborough Redburn in this seafaring tale. Redburn's arduous sea voyage – based on Melville's own first trip as an apprentice seaman – takes him from New York to Liverpool, where he is shocked by the devastating poverty he witnesses. Dreadful shipboard conditions feature in *Redburn* as they do in its follow-up novel *White-Jacket* – which was based on Melville's experiences during his final sea voyage. Here, floggings (below) and the brutal conditions endured by seamen are described in vivid, keenly felt detail. Melville described *Redburn* and *White-Jacket* (so called after the narrator's white jacket) as 'two jobs, which I have done for money – being forced to it, as other men are to sawing wood'. Yet they are compelling tales, with powerful characters, such as the 'incomparable' main top captain Jack Chase, and the evil Surgeon Cuticle.

Detail from Derby Day by W.P. Frith. Tate Gallery, London

## ISRAEL POTTER

◆ 1855 ◆

**(left) Set mainly during the American War of Independence,** this historical novel is based on the anonymous *Life and Remarkable Adventures of Israel Potter* (1824), a rather tedious factual account of patriotic adventures which Melville transforms and brings to life. Israel Potter, a restless New England boy (whose experiences happen to include a trip on a whaling ship) joins the American rebels against British rule, but is captured at Bunker Hill and taken to England as a prisoner. He escapes, and becomes an American agent. Among the historical figures whom Potter meets are the two great American heroes Benjamin Franklin (left, inset) and the naval officer John Paul Jones. As a friend of Jones, Potter is present when Jones captures the British ship the *Serapis* in 1799, in a long and bloody sea battle. Back in England, Potter escapes detection by working as a labourer. He marries and settles down for 'His Fifty Years of Exile' – the subtitle of the novel. When Potter returns to America as an old man, he applies to Congress for a pension. But his application fails, since there is no evidence of his ever having been in military service, and the old soldier dies in penury – after first dictating his memoirs.

BPCC/Aldus Archive Inset: Peter Newark's Western Americana

# The Restless Pacific

**The exotic, sensational South Seas fascinated both Melville and his readers. But the 'civilized world' seemed determined to invade, plunder and exploit this paradise. Melville witnessed the fall begin.**

**Nave Nave Mahana** *(right) 'Delightful Day' was painted in 1896 when French artist Paul Gauguin returned a second time to Tahiti. His own days were anything but delightful, governed mainly by a lack of money and bad health. He antagonized the colonials by urging the native people not to pay taxes and to take their children out of mission school, and he preached uninhibited enjoyment of life. The day after he died, a Catholic bishop visited his hut and, it is thought, destroyed all those canvases he considered obscene.*

Vast areas of the Pacific were not much explored until the 19th century. Then, as fact and rumour filtered back to the 'civilized world', images of exotic islands, strange cultures, mysterious rituals and fabulous sea creatures fired the public's imagination. The South Seas were an antidote to boredom, disillusionment and drudgery. They were the Garden of Eden rediscovered, with its gates ajar.

Novelists had been using the Pacific as a setting for their fiction since the 18th century. Daniel Defoe's *Life and Strange and Surprising Adventures of Robinson Crusoe* (1719) is Caribbean in flavour. Jonathan Swift's *Gulliver's Travels* (1726) takes place largely without reference to conventional geography, but is supposed to be set in the South Seas. Melville's contemporary, Robert Louis Stevenson went to the South Seas to live and die, and set more books there than his most famous *Treasure Island* (1883), although one critic well versed in the life of the islands wrote dismissively, 'it is positively impossible to get a single breath of ocean air from R.L.S.' Later, Joseph Conrad was to set heroes afloat on the Pacific in search of atonement or self-knowledge. But Melville alone is considered *the* novelist of the South Seas. Six of his ten novels are set there: *Typee, Omoo, Mardi, Redburn, White-Jacket, Moby-Dick*. His poems, too, published under the title *John Marr and Other Sailors*, owe a debt to his experiences among the islands.

### PEACE AND WAR

The Pacific inspired Melville as a place of contrasts – idyllic islands and terrible sea storms, innocence and cannibalism, the battle of wills between the indigenous peoples and the European missionaries. Melville the adventurer discovered in the Marquesas islands, Tahiti and Honolulu, ready-made plots for his early fiction, detail, atmosphere and symbols for *Moby-Dick*. He had started writing only months before he left America in January 1841 and his very first port of call, the Marquesas, unleashed a flood of romance eloquently recaptured at the open of *Typee*:

*"What strange vision of outlandish things does the very name spirit up! Naked houris – cannibal banquets – groves of coconut – coral-reefs – tattooed chiefs – and bamboo temples; sunny valleys planted with breadfruit-trees – carved canoes dancing on the flashing blue waters – savage woodlands guarded by horrible idols – heathenish rites and human sacrifices."*

This was an exciting world, and Melville, the first

National Maritime Museum, London

### Clothing their nakedness

*European missionaries blanched at the sight of naked women, and despite a climate entirely unsuited to layers of prudish Victorian clothing, villagers were soon dressing like the newcomers (below). They needed little persuasion. Many were so anxious to imitate the affluent Westerners that there were some errors of interpretation . . . (right).*

Gauguin: Nave Nave Mahana. Musee des Beaux-Arts, Lyon/Bridgeman Art Library

Phaidon Press

BBC Hulton Picture Library

### South Sea Islands

*(left) Amazed and appalled were those who first arrived there. The great beauty of the scenery and of the people was in sharp contrast to the violence of inter-tribal warfare and the dark menace of cannibalism and evil spirits. Reactions were mixed. Some visitors longed to throw off the chains of civilized convention and become part of island life. Some (for whom Victorian ethics and behaviour seemed the ultimate good) were bent on moulding the native culture into a shabby replica of home. Some simply saw a quick profit to be made at the islanders' expense.*

major writer to visit the area, stepped into it at just the right time.

The South Sea islands were then in political turmoil. Tahiti (Melville's second stop) had been claimed by the British in 1767, and 30 years later the London Missionary Society had established a base there to preach 'the everlasting gospel' to a people of 'mental ignorance and moral depravity'. (The 30 founders of the Society contained only four ordained ministers, the rest being made up of carpenters, hatters, butchers, tailors and so on.)

All went well until 1836, when two French Catholic missionaries arrived, disguised as carpenters, to counteract the influence of the British Protestants. They were promptly expelled by the island's queen, but the French returned, backed up by the navy. They demanded 2,000 Spanish dollars and permission to establish a garrison.

### HELD TO RANSOM

Sadly for the island's government, London was not over-concerned, despite desperate appeals for 'the shelter of her wing, the defence of her lion, and the protection of her flag'. In 1841 the Protestant missionaries had little option but to withdraw. The following year the French invaded the Marquesas, where they had been in

charge for just six weeks when Melville's ship, the *Acushnet*, anchored off-shore. There was no mistaking the atmosphere of conflict when Melville saw *"the tri-coloured flag of France trailing over the stern of six vessels, whose black hulls and bristling broadsides proclaimed their warlike character."*

In Tahiti, the island chiefs were so outraged that they trapped some of the French forces in a coastal settlement. The French retaliated by training 60 naval guns on the capital, Papeete, and demanded a further fine of 10,000 Spanish dollars. The Tahitian government submitted, and in April 1843 the island became a French protectorate.

There was some local resistance to the French led by the Reverend George Pritchard (eventually expelled) and Queen Pomare whose forces Melville thought of joining. But in the end he saved his fiercest attacks on the French for his writings.

The islanders were not only losing their political independence. Those living in coastal settlements and trading villages found their lifestyles remoulded by the missionaries. Sexual freedom, nudity, drunkenness and dancing were strenuously discouraged. Even tossing the football, kite flying and singing were deemed punishable offences, and the missionaries enforced their rules through the kannakippers (religious police).

## Sources and Inspiration

### Buccaneering adventurers

*The South Seas were already dimly associated, in Western minds, with freebooting lawlessness and swashbuckling adventure. In his stories, Robert Louis Stevenson was able to capitalize on the almost mythical appeal of such long-gone pirates as Blackbeard (left). The reality of piracy was sordid, bloody and ruthless. Melville similarly transformed his subjects – whaling, mutiny and beachcombing.*

Melville never hid his dislike for such attempts to westernize and curb the natural instincts of the islanders, though these occasionally shocked him. He wrote of 'every species of riot and debauchery' occurring on deck when the island girls swam out to greet his ship. Such scenes must have been commonplace as an increasing number of whalers and trading ships pulled in to South Sea harbours.

The missionaries tended to keep to the main villages, rarely travelling to the remoter areas for fear of being killed and eaten. Although Melville reported in *Typee* that he stayed with a tribe of cannibals, it seems he was never in any real danger of being pot-boiled. He simply realized the dramatic and commercial value of mentioning the fact. But cannibalism certainly existed.

One report of 1840 describes how 'A battle ensued between the tribes, in which two were killed upon each side, and hostilities then ceased to allow the contending parties the luxury of feeding upon their respective prisoners.' The only known eyewitness account of cannibalism comes from John Couter, a surgeon on a whaler, who wrote in 1833 how some of those killed in a tribal battle were eaten.

### SLAVERS AND TRADERS

When islanders came into conflict with White explorers, however, the islanders usually came off worse, their greatest danger being from slavers. The development of the Pacific plantations in the 1860s was founded on cheap, forced labour. The slavers' usual tactics were to anchor off-shore and wait for islanders to row out to exchange gifts. When their canoes came alongside, the sailors dropped lumps of pig iron on to the flimsy vessels, smashing and sinking them. Then they picked up the survivors and packed them into the hold.

From the start, the Australians were among the worst offenders. In 1814, the governor of New South Wales complained of the atrocities and injustices being inflicted on the South Sea Island peoples. Nearly 60 years later the *Carl* was intercepted by the British navy and 176 native islanders were discovered locked in the hold. One infamous slaver, Michael Fodger, clubbed and threw prisoners overboard once his hold was full. He was eventually killed by Tahitians whom he had intended for slavery.

Roger Viollet

**Royal houses**

*(above) The Tahitian royal household was based not in Tahiti, but on the nearby island of Ra'iaten – the centre of traditional religious worship. By the time this photograph was taken of the royal family outside the residence, Ra'iaten's religious significance had been lost. Christianity ruled on the main island.*

**A host of races**

*(left) So many different races existed in the thousands of isolated islands that the scope of their religions, ceremonies, appearance, laws, behaviour and lifestyles allowed any traveller's tale to be believed. Pygmies, cannibals and tattooed idol-worshippers could all be vouched for.*

**The scourge of slavery**

*(right) When labour was needed on the plantations, whole villages were herded into slavery. For the most part, there was no need for the kind of raiding party pictured above right, since the islanders rowed out unsuspecting to the slave-ships to exchange gifts, and were thrown into the holds.*

Mansell Collection

Another attraction of the Pacific was sweet-smelling sandalwood, which was used in Chinese religious ceremonies and the perfumery industry. When European and American traders found a rich source in Fiji, they did not stop to ask the islanders' permission, but plundered it until supplies were exhausted, before moving on to neighbouring islands.

The islands were also used as staging posts. Ships carrying seal skins from the subarctic stopped in at the Marquesas islands before sailing on to China. Sealers from the north-west American coast, also bound for China, stopped to take on food supplies at Tahiti.

The Tahitians tried to establish their own trading

fleet, sending coconut oil, pork, arrowroot, sandalwood and pearls to America, Australia and China. But they received such ruthlessly unfavourable terms that they ran at a loss. In fact the enterprise did more harm than good, depriving the villages of much needed food.

Whaling, too, helped ruin the island economies. In 1788 the British whaler *Emilia* sailed round Cape Horn and discovered an abundance of whales off the western shores of South America. This discovery, coinciding with a growing industrial need for whale oil, resulted in years of exhaustive whaling which reached its peak when Melville himself hunted whales.

The sheer number of whalers in the South Seas

**'Riot and debauchery'**
*The native women who boarded European ships at anchor were anxious to please. The common sailor after months at sea, could hardly believe his luck, though God-fearing Christians found it all rather shocking. Melville himself was shocked, but knew he was glimpsing a different culture. He was incensed when missionaries tried to curb traditional native practices. The outcome for the islanders was the worst one possible. While missionaries interfered with village life – forbidding nudity, dancing, polygamy and all sexual positions but one – the sailors were not to be denied the chief delights of an island stopover and speedily infected their hosts with VD. The disease decimated whole populations.*

inevitably increased contact between the native and Western cultures. One of the worst consequences was the introduction and uncontrollable spread of disease. The native islanders had never had to develop any resistance to diseases such as measles, mumps, jaundice, dysentery and whooping cough, and no remedies then existed to help them survive. In 1846 the estimated population of the Marquesas islands was 100,000. By 1890 it had slumped to 16,000. This was only in very small part the result of local wars. The surviving population was more devastated by a range of foreign social or cultural vices – venereal disease, opium addiction and alcohol abuse – all the direct result of Western influence. The local economy and workforce were thus decimated.

## DISILLUSIONMENT

The worst hit areas were around the main harbours, known as 'refreshments', where traders landed for sex, provisions and to go sight-seeing. Papeete in Tahiti, and Honolulu were two of the most attractive stopping-places.

This picture of a declining and ruined South Sea island people contrasts sadly with Melville's descriptions in *Typee*, of 'as polished a community as ever the sun shone upon,' so happy and contented that 'with them there hardly appeared to be any difference of opinion upon any subject whatsoever'. He witnessed

the first but not the worst effects of the White man on the South Seas.

A French naval officer, under the pseudonym Pierre Loti, sought out unspoiled corners of the South Seas and in the 1880s wrote about them in highly poetic and sentimental terms. It was he and not Melville who saw the native culture finally overwhelmed by Western influences. And he inadvertently inspired Europeans by the thousand to drop everything and seek an idyllic life among the islands – thereby ensuring a universal rout of the idyll.

It is hardly surprising to discover that when the French artist Paul Gauguin decided to go to Tahiti 50 years after Melville's visit, he had been inspired to expect an exotic, untouched island paradise. But large areas had become so westernized that 65,000 gallons of claret were being imported each year. There were church bells and gendarmes, French housewives and hierarchy. 'It was Europe all over again' Gauguin wrote, 'just what I thought I had broken away from – made still worse by colonial snobbery'.

Melville saw enough to understand that the South Seas were a place of beauty and conflict, and there can be no doubting the Pacific's hold over him. The 'tide-beating heart of Earth' with its 'milky ways of coral isles', which he describes in *Moby-Dick*, nourished both his imagination and the distinctive moral vision that made him one of America's finest writers.

# JOSEPH CONRAD

## ►1857-1924◄

Józef Korzeniowski left his native Poland for the tough,
adventurous life of a merchant seaman. He survived shipwreck
and attempted suicide before coming to England – where he
settled to writing of his past experiences in a foreign language
for an indifferent public. Despite illness, poverty and a
constitutional pessimism, Conrad was true to his new calling
and by it achieved fame as the finest foreign ambassador of the
English novel.

# HOME FROM THE SEA

**Escaping a bleak childhood for adventure on sunlit seas, Conrad finally settled in a new country to a new career. But he could never outrun the deep pessimism that was his inheritance.**

Many aspiring novelists have courted adventure in order to fire their imagination. Joseph Conrad was one lucky exception. He did not start writing until he was 32, or become a full-time writer until he was 39, by which time he had seen more than most people do in a lifetime. He had been involved in gun-running, had tried to kill himself, had left a secure home for a tough life at sea, and had travelled to Europe, Asia, Australia and the Far East. Further voyages of his, particularly to Africa, left his fellow novelist Henry James marvelling, 'No one has *known* . . . the things you know.' Even more impressive was the manner in which Conrad converted these experiences into half-a-dozen brilliant novels, all written in a language he did not learn until he was 20.

Joseph Conrad (or Józef Teodor Konrad Korzeniowski, as he was christened) was born on 3 December 1857 into an aristocratic Polish family. His father Apollo influenced him in three significant ways. As a patriot fighting the Russians, who had annexed Poland, Apollo passed on his hatred of Russia. He also bequeathed to Józef a love for literature – and a profound pessimism.

Being born into an aristocratic Polish family did not mean privilege. In 1861 Apollo was arrested for being politically dangerous and was exiled, with his family, to northern Russia. Here Conrad got his first taste of a deprived, joyless world. Apollo's description of it could have come from one of his son's novels: 'everything [is] rotting and shifting under one's feet . . . The population is a nightmare: disease-ridden corpses'. His wife Eva was the first to succumb to the murderous climate and died four years later. In later life Józef vener-

***Exiled and orphaned***
*Conrad (centre) was born at Berdyczow (below left), in the part of Poland under Russian domination. When he was three, his parents were exiled to northern Russia for their nationalist activities. Conrad's mother, Eva (top), whom he later revered as 'the ideal of Polish womanhood', died three years later. Father and son were allowed to return to Cracow (below) in 1869, but father Apollo died shortly after and the 11-year-old Józef was left an orphan.*

ated her photograph as if it were a religious icon.

For the next three years Apollo, despite his own sickness and poverty, tried to shield Conrad from 'the atmosphere of this place', but it was largely in vain. Conrad grew up 'as though in a monastic cell', repeatedly falling ill. Even worse, Apollo now had terminal consumption and although his sentence was repealed in 1868, enabling them to head south for Cracow, it was too late. Apollo died four months later. According to one biographer, Conrad was in 'inconsolable despair'.

## BREAKING FREE

The parental gap was filled by Conrad's uncle Thadeus to whom he 'quickly became devoted.' Thadeus saw education as the key to Conrad's success but he had a difficult task convincing the boy. Another relative wrote that while Conrad 'was intellectually well developed, he hated the rigours of school . . . he used to say that he had a great talent and would become a great writer.'

By the time Conrad was 15, it was getting harder to keep him in school. Prompted by his love of adventure stories and the threat of being conscripted into the Russian army, he pleaded to be allowed to go to sea. For two years Thadeus tried to dissuade him, but at last he relented.

Conrad was based in Marseilles for the next four

*Mary Evans Picture Library*

### On the waterfront
*To escape the threat of military service in the Russian army, and in pursuit of the adventure he had read about, young Conrad (inset) went to Marseilles (above) and became a sailor. Here, difficulty with getting work, abortive attempts at making money and, perhaps, an unhappy love affair reduced Conrad to such despair that he attempted suicide. His faithful Uncle Thadeus redeemed his bad debts, and set the unstable youth on a steadier course – for England and more seafaring.*

## Key Dates

**1857** born in Russian-annexed Poland

**1862** family banished to northern Russia

**1865** mother dies

**1869** father dies

**1874** goes to Marseilles

**1877** attempts suicide

**1878** enters British Merchant Navy

**1886** gains British citizenship and Master's certificate

**1889** begins writing

**1895** goes to Belgian Congo

**1896** marries Jessie George

**1900** *Lord Jim*

**1914** visits Poland

**1924** declines knighthood; dies in Kent

wild years. In addition to sailing to the West Indies, he ran through his generous allowance, and further difficulties arose when an irregularity with his work permit ruled out any more voyages. Conrad tried to make a quick fortune by smuggling, but instead lost 3,000 francs in the enterprise. He then borrowed a further 800 which he promptly lost in the gambling rooms at Monte Carlo. In utter despair Conrad attempted suicide. The bullet was aimed at his heart – but missed. This was the first experience of his to be repeatedly used in his novels; he wrote a total of nine fictional suicides, and three of his characters throw their lives away.

Thadeus came to his financial rescue, and 22-year-old Conrad left Marseilles for England, even though he could barely speak six words of the language. From here he continued his seafaring life. Restless and reckless as ever, he repeatedly quarrelled with various captains on trips to the Mediterranean and Australia.

During Conrad's voyages he studied for naval exams and when he was 30 gained his Master's certificate, which enabled him to captain ships. Though he regarded this as a personal triumph – 'vindicating myself' – he was actually growing disillusioned with life at sea, 'sailing for little money and consideration', and was tempted to become a businessman. He was also nearing the point when he would leap into a third, different world – that of the novelist. A lover of all things British – the language, the politics, the freedom – he was naturalized in 1886.

### JOURNEY INTO HELL

Conrad had been to the Far East on voyages out of Marseilles, but his first real opportunity to study the area and its people came in 1887, when a back injury forced him into hospital for three months in Singapore. On his recovery, he explored the city, 'riotous with life', and spent four and a half months touring the nearby islands.

Conrad returned to London in 1889. He had had a score of adventures but was penniless and without a real career. Although he had never attempted to write anything longer than a letter, and that usually in French, he began his first novel, *Almayer's Folly*. In 1889 he returned to Poland to visit Thadeus and on the way became involved with Marguerite Poradowska, a woman 10 years older than himself and the widow of his cousin. They struck up an immediate friendship, regularly corresponding with each other over the next few years, often about his writings. It was even rumoured that Conrad proposed to her. She found him a new post and organized his next voyage, which was to prove the most important and difficult of his life – to Africa, up the Congo, into the "heart of darkness".

### Shipboard meeting
*While first mate of the* Torrens *(right), Conrad met John Galsworthy (centre). They spurred each other into writing careers and remained lifelong friends.*

Conrad knew it would be a dangerous journey because he was replacing a young river-steamer captain who had just been murdered by Africans. Even after three months the man was 'still unburied – his hands and feet had been cut off – his clothes taken away . . .' It was a journey into hell. For Conrad, sailing upstream in a 'tin-pot' steamer "was like travelling back to the earliest beginnings of the world, when vegetation rioted on the earth and the big trees were kings . . ." The crew was racked with dysentery and fever, the Europeans suffering the most. The end of the river journey, later brilliantly recaptured in Conrad's masterly novel *Heart of Darkness*, was no Romantic communion with nature, but a terrifying vision of "the vilest scramble for loot". The Europeans were after ivory and no-one was allowed to get in their way.

Conrad went down with acute fever and was prematurely forced back to England. In London he remained in hospital for six weeks, and he was left a prey to malarial gout which intermittently

attacked him for the rest of his life, giving him severe pain.

Conrad's pessimism, fuelled by the Congo journey, increased when Thadeus died in 1894. He gave up the sea and turned to writing, his first task being to finish *Almayer's Folly*. The book won good reviews, as did his follow-up, *An Outcast of the Islands*, and this good fortune was matched by an upturn in his personal life.

## A MARRIED MAN

In 1896 Conrad married Jessie George, a typist 16 years younger than himself. Though some questioned his choice, the couple complemented each other well, her calm, placid personality offsetting his restless, intense, highly-strung temperament. Married life began in rugged, remote Britanny, where he wrote and she typed out the manuscripts, but malarial gout and depression drove Conrad back to Essex the following year, where he began work on *The Rescuer* and finished

**Foreign ports**
*Conrad sailed all over the world – to Australasia, Martinique, Haiti, Colombia and the West Indies (left), though half his time was spent on shore between voyages.*

**Master mariner**
*(right) In 1886, at the second attempt, Conrad gained his Master's Certificate, enabling him to captain a ship. His most fateful journey – deep into the Belgian Congo – still awaited him.*

## GUN-RUNNING TO RUIN

Stranded penniless in Marseilles, young Conrad, in desperation, joined a rebel group intent on returning the deposed monarch, Don Carlos, to the Spanish throne. They were sea-going gun-runners, smuggling weapons to the Royalists. On their last voyage, they were pursued by the coastguard and, to avoid capture, wrecked their boat against the rocky coast. Conrad recounted later how he 'and the other smugglers had hidden for days in a low *posada* [inn], in an underground cellar . . . till the authorities had given up the search'. He wrote many fictionalized accounts of the incident: in *The Mirror of the Sea*, *The Arrow of Gold* and *The Sisters*. Some suggest he fell in love with the beautiful leader of the group, Doña Rita. She could even have been the real cause of his subsequent suicide bid.

his long seafaring tale, *The Nigger of the 'Narcissus'*.

As a new author, Conrad worked extremely hard wrestling out his narratives. Lack of money was to be an abiding problem for most of his writing life, but such anxieties were tempered by having a quiet, comfortable, rural home and good friends. He rented a farmhouse – Pent Farm in Kent – from fellow writer Ford Madox Ford from 1898 to 1907, and this brought him into contact with a group of major authors including H.G. Wells, Henry James, Rudyard Kipling and Stephen Crane, who lived nearby.

Conrad had stipulated as a condition of his marriage to Jessie that they would have no children – but a son, Borys, was born in 1898. Conrad was not always the dutiful father. On one notorious occasion he disowned the bawling baby and his mother on a train journey, going to sit at the far end of the carriage. But he and Borys came in time to have as close and important a relationship as he had enjoyed with Thadeus. Meanwhile Conrad wrote some of his finest novels at Pent Farm, producing *Lord Jim, Heart of Darkness, Youth,* and many short stories, while continuing to struggle with *The Rescuer,* growling, 'I'm powerless to invent a way out of it'.

### PLUNGING FORTUNES

After six good years at the farm, events turned against Conrad. *Nostromo*, the novel on which he had placed enormous financial and literary hopes, got the 'blackest possible frost' from the public. The strain of writing made him ill, while Jessie had her own misfortune, being semi-crippled after injuring her knee. With money already scarce, a banking disaster which lost him part of his savings sent him 'really out of my mind with worry . . . My nerves are all to pieces.' However, a secret government grant of £500 helped alleviate the fearful gloom.

Conrad's next work – *The Secret Agent* (begun in 1905) – was an attempt to hit the best-seller list. But given his complex structuring and weighty prose, it was never likely to be a major success. Conrad despaired when he compared its proceeds with the money being earned by dull, second-rate writers. Moreover his need for financial security had been increased by the birth of a second son. Although his literary agent gave him financial help, he could not prevent Conrad's imminent breakdown. A reporter sent to interview him at this time noted: 'He is abnormally highly strung. He is sensitive, intensely susceptible to any slight jarring influences from outside. His nerves seem to be all on end.'

One symptom of Conrad's worsening state was his increased restlessness. Between 1907 and 1910 the family moved three times. In addition he fell out with his friend Ford Madox Ford, and had such a violent row with his agent that he returned home and collapsed. His wife wrote: 'Months of nervous strain have ended in a complete nervous breakdown. Poor Conrad is very ill . . . [his manuscript is] on a table at the foot of his bed and

Marianne North: View of the Salak Volcano, Java. Royal Botanic Gardens, Kew

Harry Ransom Humanities Research Center, University of Texas at Austin

he lives mixed up in the scenes and holds converse with the characters.'

### AN IRONIC TURN

Gradually he recovered, but his pessimism became awesome. He rejected the possibility of improving the world; it was foolish vanity even to consider it. To him, life was a pointless machine, a 'chaos of scraps of iron' in which nothing mattered because there was only one end, 'cold darkness and silence'. Ironically, at the very time that Conrad's most creative period ended, he won the financial gains he had so longed for. He was paid a good price for his manuscripts, received a Civil Pension,

*Inspiring encounters*
As a British merchant seaman, Conrad's travels took him to the Far East (above) where he made acquaintance with those exotic characters who would appear later in his novels.

*Married life*
Though temperamentally Conrad's opposite, Jessie George (left) proved an ideal, placid wife. Despite his wish to be childless, Jessie bore him two sons whom he came to adore. From 1919 the family (right) lived in relative comfort at a house called 'Oswalds' (below), near Canterbury.

© Canterbury Heritage Museum

and *Chance* (which he had deliberately given a more palatable, softened ending) became a hit on both sides of the Atlantic.

In 1914 Conrad made a victorious return to Poland, but the outbreak of World War I forced him and his family back to England. He enthusiastically joined in the war effort, making guest visits to secret naval bases on the East coast, where he stirred the young men to greater resolve by telling stories of danger and glory. But he quickly became disillusioned by this 'nightmare' war. When it was over, he rounded off 23 years of intermittent work on one novel by completing *The Rescuer* (published as *The Rescue*). And he sold the film rights to his works for £4000.

### 'I AM FINISHED'

When Conrad was 66 he made his first trip to America as one of Britain's most distinguished authors. But he was a reluctant celebrity, shunning 40 press photographers waiting on the quayside. The talks he gave tended to be private ones rather than public lectures; one of the most impressive lasting for nearly three hours. Despite his bad pronunciation ('good' sounded like 'gut', 'blood' like 'blut') the audience was hypnotized as he read of the death of one of his heroines, until his voice broke and he 'was moved to sudden tears'.

## ABANDON SHIP!

The steamship *Jeddah* sailed from Singapore in July 1880 carrying over 1,000 Muslim pilgrims. On 8 August, during a storm, it began to take water. Captain Clark set the crew to working the pumps, but rumour spread that the lifeboats were leaving. Chief Officer A.P. Williams, to save his skin, told Clark the passengers meant to murder his wife. Clark took his wife and European officers and boarded the lifeboats. They were picked up and taken to Aden where Clark reported the ship lost. Next day, another steamer towed the *Jeddah* safe into port. Legal judgement called it 'the most extraordinary instance . . . of the abandonment of a disabled and leaking ship'. But Clark's ticket was merely suspended for three years; most blame was put on Williams. Many believe Conrad met Williams – who was certainly one model for Jim. But in a Borneo trading post in 1887, Conrad met young Jim Lingard, known locally as 'Tuan Jim', who fleshed out the fictional hero.

Back in England came two honours. He sat for the great sculptor, Jacob Epstein, and was offered a knighthood, which he rejected. But his end was near. Epstein commented at the time that he 'was crippled with rheumatism, crotchety and ill. He has said to me, "I am finished." ' Years of worry and malarial gout had taken their toll. After a heart attack in June 1924 Conrad confided: 'I begin to feel like a cornered rat'. Shortly after came the second attack. He told his sons, 'You know I am very ill this time'. The next morning, 3 August 1924, he collapsed and died.

The epitaph engraved on the tombstone of one of the greatest 20th-century writers was chosen by the man himself. It was a quotation from the eminently English, Elizabethan poet Edmund Spenser, and it was particularly apt:

*Sleep after toyle, port after stormie sea,*
*Ease after warre, death after life, does greatly please.*

Dodd, Mead & Company, Inc.

59

# LORD JIM

**Professional misconduct and personal disgrace send Jim to the most far-flung places on a quest for peace and redemption.**

Conrad began *Lord Jim* as a short story, developing it gradually into one of this century's most richly complex novels about what motivates human action, particularly in times of crisis. It is a demanding read, but infinitely rewarding; Conrad's exploration of Jim's inner journey to find a way of living at peace with himself is filled with universal truths. The novel invites us to empathize with the emotional confusion that cripples Jim, suggesting that we follow the story and reserve judgement at least until we have examined our own hearts and minds.

## GUIDE TO THE PLOT

Jim, the son of a morally upright English parson, goes to sea charged with a romantic, youthful desire to perform great acts of heroism. His first, brief taste of failure comes when, as a naval cadet, he hesitates to join a rescue party. They put out from the ship without him, and he is left to nurse his disappointment, imagining himself the hero of far greater courageous exploits at some hazy point in the future.

Jim takes a commission as first mate on the *Patna*, a rusty old ship severely overloaded with 800 muslim pilgrims. Sailing through the waters of the Far East, the

### Lost at sea
*On a calm sea in the dead of night (right), the* Patna *strikes a submerged object – "She went over whatever it was as easy as a snake crawling over a stick". On duty-watch and surrounded by a cargo of sleeping humanity, Jim foresees imminent death. But something much worse awaits him.*

### The runner
*His naval career at an end, Jim works as a water-clerk (below) – a runner for chandlers in a succession of foreign ports. But his story pursues him, driving him to increasingly remote places in search of anonymity.*

Alexander Stanhope Forbes: The Lighthouse. City of Manchester Art Galleries

Aiwasowski: Night on the Black Sea. Kunstmuseum, Odessa

D. Maxwell: Port of Aden/Mary Evans Picture Library

> *"He stood still looking at these recumbent bodies, a doomed man aware of his fate, surveying the silent company of the dead. They <u>were</u> dead! Nothing could save them!… No time! No time! It did not seem worth while to open his lips, to stir hand or foot."*

boat strikes a submerged object. Convinced the hull will cave in at any minute, the crew panic and decide to save themselves without alerting the passengers. Knowing that the lifeboats cannot possibly accommodate 800 people, Jim is disgusted by their cowardice. He decides to remain on board and go down with the ship. At the very last moment, however, barely conscious of his actions, he jumps and deserts ship with the others. Rescued later, Jim and the crew learn that the *Patna* did not sink, but was towed to safety by a French gunboat.

Determined to face the consequences of his behaviour, Jim endures a lengthy trial which strips him of his dignity and his licence to sail. Marlow, an observer at the inquiry, becomes fascinated with Jim's heroic bearing and makes it his business to find out more about this unusual young man. Marlow decides to help Jim make a new start. He sets him up with a job, but the notoriety of the *Patna* affair follows Jim from port to port, making it impossible for him to stay in any line of work for very long. Still anxious to help Jim settle, Marlow contacts an old friend called Stein, who manages to find a post for Jim in a

settlement called Patusan. So remote is this place that, once Jim is there, "it would be for the outside world as though he had never existed."

Armed with an unloaded revolver and with his dreams of glory still intact, Jim arrives in Patusan and in an astonishingly short period manages to win the trust and loyalty of the community, who name him 'Tuan Jim' meaning 'Lord Jim'. He falls in love with a native girl called Jewel, and it seems his happiness should be complete. But even Patusan is not immune from outside influences and the ultimate test of character is still in store for Jim.

## VOYAGE OF THE SOUL

Conrad's *Lord Jim* has all the ingredients of a fine adventure story set in distant high seas. It is filled with extraordinary characters, promising drama, romance and tragedy from beginning to end. He began writing the novel as a serial published in monthly parts for *Blackwood's Magazine* in 1899/1900. Absorbed by the development of its hero, Conrad kept writing, and produced a novel far longer than had originally been commissioned, and certainly of much greater weight and

P. S. Kroyer: Figures in a Tavern/Fine Art Photographic Library

### Witnesses
*Jim's trial takes place in a middle-Eastern port – probably Aden (left). Here Marlow meets the* Patna's *chief engineer (above), who is deranged by drink. In his nightmare delusions, he recalls the ship's sleeping passengers as a million pink, knotting toads.*

---

fascination than a mere adventure story.

In a letter dated 1895 he explained some of his views on the purpose of fiction: 'Imagination . . . should be used to create human souls: to disclose human hearts – and not to create events that are properly speaking *accidents* only.' In *Lord Jim* Con-rad's concern was not to tell an eventful tale so much as to analyze, with extraordinary detail and sensitivity, the heart and soul of his central character Jim. The reasons why Jim behaves as he does are far more significant than what he actually does in the course of the book.

Conrad strives to create a character with whom we can sympathize and in whom we can become sufficiently interested to seek answers to the book's eternal questions. By giving the narration of the story to Marlow, the ageing, experienced captain, Conrad allows himself a voice in the novel. What we know of Jim is revealed through Marlow's observations and insights. Marlow narrates the events to a group of friends over one long evening, skipping backwards and forwards in time, and blurring the sequence in order to explore what really interests him: Jim's essential character

**Malayan sanctuary**
*(right) "Thirty miles of forest shut it off from the sight of an indifferent world, and the noise of the white surf along the coast overpowered the voice of fame." The charitable German, Stein, believing in Jim's essential merit, finds him a post in this remote Malay archipelago where the young man rewards his trust many times over.*

"The first to believe in him"
*(left) Jim finds a friend in Dain Waris. But their mutual "courage in the open" proves fatal.*

Mary Evans Picture Library

*"Man is amazing, but he is not a masterpiece . . . Sometimes it seems to me that man is come where he is not wanted, where there is no place for him; for if not, why should he want all the place? Why should he run about here and there making a great noise about himself, talking about the stars, disturbing the blades of grass?"*

**Evil interloper**
*Tribal dissent and petty jealousy explode into violence when the pirate Gentleman Brown moors off Patusan.*

traits and the reasons for his downfall.

However, Marlow's reliability as a narrator is repeatedly questioned. He admits at times that, "It is impossible to see him clearly", and "I cannot say I had ever seen him distinctly – not even to this day, after I had my last view of him." He describes his impressions of Jim as "glimpses through the shifting rents in a thick fog – bits of vivid and vanishing detail, giving no connected idea . . ."

Marlow becomes as important a character as Jim himself, with his reflections on Jim's psyche as well as on the state of humankind in general. Indeed, all the characters who appear in the book, however briefly, have a role to play in disclosing aspects of the human condition. Nothing in the novel is incidental. All the seemingly shapeless fragments of conversation and description systematically intersect to illuminate Jim's motives and actions, and offer verdicts on his worth as a human being.

## COWARDICE AND COURAGE

Almost the entire novel is focused on the significance of the jump that Jim makes from the *Patna* to the lifeboat that contains the fleeing crew, whom he professes to despise. He is not like them; as Conrad

G. Hawkins · H. M. S. Dido at Sarawak. British Library/Bridgeman Art Library

*Marianne North: Sarawak. Royal Botanic Gardens, Kew*

what has happened is much more to do with having failed to live out his dream. His sense of shame and disgrace is heightened by his obsession with what might have been, had he stayed on the ship. Desperate to claw back his self-esteem he determines to face things out by staying for the Inquiry, when his fellow crew members have cut and run. By way of atonement, Jim displays a certain moral courage both at this point, and later on. But it is a frighteningly rigid kind of courage, the kind which prevents him from ever really facing himself.

## DROWNING IN DREAMS

We are offered the conclusion that courage born of self-delusion is of no use to a man. Jim will never be at peace until he learns to live with himself – " . . . running. Absolutely running with nowhere to go to", Jim imagines himself always to be something other than he is. Even in Patusan, where he achieves the glory and love to which he has always aspired, he is still, in the final analysis, unable to distinguish between good and evil.

It is Stein, the ageing butterfly collector, steeped in wisdom from a lifetime of adventuring, who gropes for the words to explain Jim's condition: "A man that is born falls into a dream like a man who falls into the sea. If he tries to climb out into the air . . . he drowns . . . The way is to the destructive element submit yourself . . ." We need real courage to accept ourselves as we are, flawed and imperfect, and to be prepared to submit to "the dream", the vagaries of life.

says in his preface, Jim 'was one of us', yet his irreversible act of cowardice literally lands him in the same boat as these treacherous rogues. Jim tries to explain his actions, but no-one at the trial is interested. The facts alone concern the audience. It is Marlow, with his desire to discover "the only truth worth knowing", who listens to Jim, admitting "the mystery of his attitude got hold of me . . ."

Jim begins his life at sea filled with a romantic idealism, imagining himself "saving people from sinking ships, cutting away masts in a hurricane . . . always an example of devotion to duty, and as unflinching as a hero in a book." But confronted with real danger, he panics and fails to live up to his ideals, breaking the fundamental moral code that says an officer should stay with his ship.

It is this betrayal of honour that disturbs Brierly, the upright Captain who sits on the Inquiry, and the French Lieutenant from whom Marlow seeks an opinion. Both acknowledge the simple fact that all men may be afraid. They recognize fear and cowardice as legitimate feelings, but believe that fulfilling one's duty and setting an example to others should finally prevail over base instinct: "a decent man would not have behaved

like this to a full cargo of old rags in bales."

As Marlow comments, "the real significance of a crime is in its being a breach of faith with the community of mankind." It becomes clear that Jim never fully understands this. His despair over

*G. Ellis H. M. S. Conway. Private Collection*

---

*In the Background*

# FROM SAIL TO STEAM

Young Jim is a cadet aboard a "training ship for officers of the mercantile marine", meaning that he was a 'Conway Boy'. Conrad, a merchant seaman himself, would have been well acquainted with *HMS Conway,* a naval college esteemed worldwide for the calibre of its officer-graduates. The *Conway* became a 20th-century anachronism, continuing to train boys under sail 50 years after the last sailing ships gave way to steam. Conrad was similarly old-fashioned in refusing to make the switch from sail to steam. Sickening early of the sea (perhaps because of the passing of sail), he was never obliged to adapt, but many skippers were made redundant by the coming of steam.

63

# CHARACTERS IN FOCUS

*Lord Jim* is peopled with diverse and eccentric characters, most of whom make a brief appearance only to fade into the obscurity of some foreign port. Essentially they fall into two groups: rogues and men of honour. Each has some bearing on the life of the hero; each reveals some aspect of Jim's nature and dilemma in telling his (or her) individual story. All are modelled on the people Conrad met during his years at sea.

## WHO'S WHO

**Jim** — The youthful hero, whose inability to live with his imperfections leads to disaster.

**Marlow** — The narrator, unable to rest in his effort to understand Jim and to explain his downfall.

**Stein** — A wise old trader with "an intrepidity of spirit", who dares to gamble on Jim's trustworthiness.

**Cornelius** — Bitter, thwarted and dangerous, he loses his post on Patusan to Jim – and determines to blight the young man's new life there.

**Gentleman Brown** — A latterday pirate driven by a "natural senseless ferocity". He intends to pillage and terrorize the inhabitants of Patusan.

**Big Brierly** — One of the assessors at Jim's trial, who "had never in his life made a mistake". He is thrown into confusion by Jim's act of cowardice.

**The French Lieutenant** — An investigating officer put aboard the *Patna* to discover how and why it was abandoned by its crew. His quiet courage is in sharp contrast to Jim's emotional turmoil.

**The Doramin** — The Malay leader on Patusan, ". . . imposing, monumental . . . a display of dignity".

**Jewel** — Jim's Malayan 'wife'.

**Tamb' Itam** — Jim's "grim and faithful retainer", son of the Doramin.

*Jewel's "youth, her ignorance, her pretty beauty,* which had the simple charm and the delicate vigour of a wild flower" (right) contrast with her passionate, jealous devotion to Jim and her agonizing fear that he will one day leave her. When Marlow meets her in the strange unsuitable setting of Stein's house, she recalls Jim bitterly: "When I used to sit at his feet, with my cheek against his knee and his hand on my head, the curse of cruelty and madness was already within him, waiting for the day. The day came! . . ."

Frederick Cayley Robinson: The 'Spirit' 'Water'. Fine Art Society/Bridgeman Art Library

*Jim (left) is eternally boyish, his thoughts "full of valorous deeds* . . . There was nothing he could not face". Physically he inspires great confidence. Marlow knows him for "one of us", and to the people of Patusan, "He appeared like a creature not only of another kind but of another essence. Had they not seen him come up in a canoe they might have thought he had descended upon them from the clouds." But Jim's nature is fatally flawed.

Richard Hook

**Cornelius (left) is the epitome of evil** – mean, abject, vicious, treacherous. "His slow laborious walk resembled the creeping of a repulsive beetle . . . perpetually slinking away". Displaced from power by Jim's arrival on Patusan, his wickedness is fuelled by jealousy of this bright, upright but vulnerable newcomer.

**Stein (right) sees in Jim echoes of himself** as a young man. Thoughtful, generous and, above all, compassionate, he alone identifies the root of Jim's troubles: "every time he shuts his eyes he sees himself as a very fine fellow – so fine as he can never be". Stein has left behind his days of sea-going adventure and now lives with his butterflies in an old age made secure by self-knowledge.

Frederick Cayley Robinson: The Day of Rest (detail), Bury Art Gallery, Lancashire/Bridgeman Art Library

**The observer of Jim's rise and fall – Marlow** (below) – is far from impartial. But his fondness for Jim, his rambling philosophical comments and self-doubt make him all the more endearing. "Many times, in distant parts of the world, Marlow showed himself willing to remember Jim . . . at length, in detail and audibly."

J. F. Raffaelli: The Father Alcazia. Museum Boymans van Beuningen, Rotterdam/Bridgeman Art Library

**Gentleman Brown** possesses "undisguised ruthlessness of purpose, a strange vengeful attitude towards his own past, and a blind belief in the righteousness of his will." Killing and robbing gratify him. But like Jim he is fleeing his past.

Peter Menim

# PLUMBING THE DEPTHS

**Writing was no easy option for Conrad. He used his experiences at sea to draw out life's hidden meaning, forging novels of extraordinary beauty in a foreign language.**

Joseph Conrad claimed with some justice that he drifted into authorship 'line by line, rather than page by page'. He began his first book, *Almayer's Folly*, in 1889, while on shore waiting for a new berth; took it up again in Switzerland three years later, while he was convalescing after his shattering experiences in the Congo; and finished it in England in 1894. But the book was not to be his only one: Conrad had begun a new novel even while waiting on tenterhooks to hear the verdict on the first – a decision which took three interminable months.

Thanks to two perceptive publisher's readers – one of them the distinguished Edward Garnett – *Almayer's Folly* was

accepted. Conrad received exactly £20 as an outright payment for the book; but he was fairly launched as a writer. However, it was only after beginning his third novel that he formally abandoned the idea of going back to sea.

Occasionally, Conrad did admit that his work brought him joy: 'I am old and sick and in debt – but lately I've found I can still write – *it* comes! *it* comes! – and I am young and healthy and rich.' But, more characteristically, he described writing as agony: 'I can't eat – I dream – nightmares – and scare my wife. I wish it was over!'

His difficulties must have been compounded by the fact that he was not writ-

**Apprentices**
*(right) One of Conrad's duties as chief officer – echoed by Marlow in* Lord Jim – *was the supervision of apprentices. Conrad looked after his 'bewildered little shavers' like a father.*

**Narrative device**
*(below) Using a method of storytelling employed by Henry James, Conrad often made Marlow his narrator: "* . . . *and with the very first word uttered Marlow's body, extended at rest in the seat, would become very still, as though his spirit had winged its way back into the lapse of time and were speaking through his lips."*

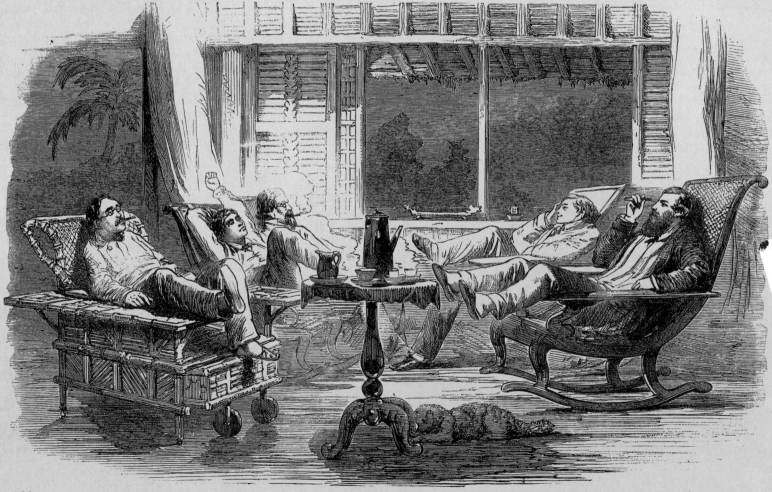

**Literary likeness**
*On the publication of Almayer's Folly, Conrad was likened to Rudyard Kipling (right), another documenter of the Far East.*

**Ford Madox Ford**
*Conrad and the garrulous Ford Madox Ford (far right) worked well together. Ford maintained that his friend thought in Polish, turned it into French, then translated it into English.*

**'Love and jealousy'**
*Methuen published* Victory *(right) in 1915. Its theme was proclaimed on the spine as 'love and jealousy'. Below is the first page of the novel in manuscript form.*

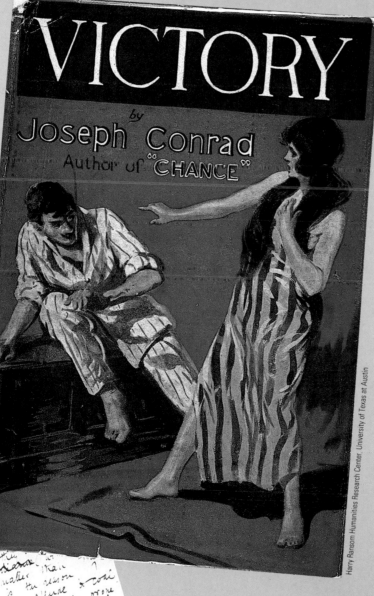

ing in his native tongue. As late as 1907 he remarked that 'English is . . . still a foreign language to me, demanding "*un effort formidable*" ', and he described his labours as 'hauling English sentences out of a black night.' But this could not have been the main obstacle, since Conrad was capable of writing quite quickly. The real problem was that he was subject to frequent writing blocks – periods when his creative faculty seemed utterly paralyzed. 'I sit down regularly every morning. I sit down for eight hours every day – and the sitting is all. In the course of that working day of 8 hours I write 3 sentences which I erase before leaving the table in despair.' As a result, some projects lingered on for years, being laid aside and taken up again several times. The record was held by *The Rescuer*, begun in 1896, which Conrad finally completed and published (as *The Rescue*) in 1920.

## DESPERATE FINANCES

Dwelling on his writing blocks, his ill health, and his desperate need for money, Conrad's letters are not a good advertisement for the literary life. Although his subjects – the sea, the East, Africa – were the very stuff of romance, wide popularity eluded him for the first 18 years of his career. He supplemented his meagre income from novels by writing for magazines, notably *Blackwood's*, and by collaborating with a younger novelist, Ford Madox Ford. Their joint novels, *The Inheritors* (1901) and *Romance* (1903), were based mainly on material supplied by Ford.

As far as his most serious work was concerned, Conrad refused to compromise – except in choice of subject. *The*

**The Arrow of Gold**
*A talented artist as well as writer, Conrad sometimes designed the dust covers of his books. On the left is his preliminary drawing for* The Arrow of Gold, *published in 1919.*

**High praise**
*The grand claim of 'greatest living artist in English prose' was made about Conrad by his publishers, Fisher Unwin, in their collected edition of his novels (1923).*

worlds. Apparently, while he was tackling his monumental work *Nostromo*, an unfortunate lady visitor accidentally stumbled into his study. Conrad leapt up, 'stunned and dazed, every nerve quivering with the pain of being uprooted out of one world and flung down in another.'

## DISTINGUISHED ADMIRERS

Although his material was very often 'romantic', Conrad's sophisticated treatment of it – his pervasive irony, his technique of shifting backwards and forwards in time, often ignoring the most 'thrilling' moment in a narrative – disconcerted contemporary readers and restricted his appeal to a relatively small literary élite.

A number of critics and fellow-novelists, such as Edward Garnett, John Galsworthy, H. G. Wells and Rudyard Kipling, recognized that Conrad was a great writer, but he was not widely read until an admirer persuaded the proprietor of the *New York Herald* to serialize *Chance*, with immediate, sensational consequences. Ironically, Conrad became rich and famous in Britain and the United States

*Secret Agent*, for example, was based on a real incident (in 1894 an anarchist named Martial Bourdin had accidentally blown himself up in Greenwich Park) which Conrad hoped would make the book popular. When this failed to happen, he speculated that there must be 'something in me that is unsympathetic to the general public . . . Foreignness, I suppose.' After all, Hardy's novels were just as tragic in outlook as his own, yet they sold well enough . . .

### INTO THE 'DARKNESS'

Conrad's philosophy was undeniably bleak. In a meaningless universe, civilization represented a definite achievement – but one that was temporary, frail and constantly under threat. The same was true of human virtues, especially when the 'good' man or woman departed from the well-lighted places of civilization. Jim, Kurtz (in *Heart of Darkness*), Nostromo, and Razumov (in *Under Western Eyes*) are all men with admirable qualities whose downfall comes about because they venture into savage places or are drawn into extreme situations that reveal their lack of inner strength.

The importance of seafaring and its code in Conrad's thought emerges in his conclusion in *Heart of Darkness*: "there is nothing in the world to hold on to but the work that has to be done on each succeeding day. Outside that there is nothing . . .

but what each man can find in himself." Although Marlow is powerfully drawn to Kurtz, the difference between them is that Marlow has a boat that must be steered – and in the heart of darkness, that is the key to sanity and survival.

In Conrad's eyes, the novelist's calling was as arduous as the seaman's. All art was 'a single-minded attempt to render the highest kind of justice to the visible universe, by bringing to light the truth . . . underlying its every aspect.' 'The artist descends within himself' in order to make the 'rescued fragment' of life 'disclose its inspiring secret'. And so, although Conrad often incorporated real people and events into his novels, he reworked them to bring out the hidden meanings he perceived in them. A work of art, he declared, usually had more than one meaning, and 'the nearer it approaches art, the more it acquires a symbolic character'.

It was this high conception of his art that made writing such a torment, since Conrad strove for 'the perfect blending of form and substance' and imposed on himself 'an unremitting . . . care for the shape and ring of sentences'.

His commitment to his task demanded a single-mindedness of purpose that extended even to his surroundings. He insisted, for example, that there be no sound whatsoever while he was writing, lest it broke the spell of his imaginary

*The greatest living artist in English prose*

just when his talent was beginning to decline, and his mostly inferior later works sold in huge numbers. It was left to a later generation, better attuned to Conrad's philosophy and 'modernist' literary approach, to give him the enduring popularity appropriate to a writer of classic status.

Conrad's experience of the sea and of exotic places permeate his novels – tales of high adventure that are also profound meditations on the human situation. His first two books, *Almayer's Folly* (1895) and *An Outcast of the Islands* (1896), are set in the romantic 'Eastern Archipelago' and display an impressive mastery of the English language. With *The Nigger of the*

*'Narcissus'* (1897) Conrad entered his most creative period; this story, *Youth* (1902) and *Typhoon* (1902) form a classic trio of sea stories. *Heart of Darkness* (1902) and the much more ambitious *Lord Jim* (1900) also focus on the idealist overmatched by circum-

stances. In *Nostromo* (1904) he creates an imaginary Central American republic. Commonplace domesticity and the underworld of politics become enmeshed in *The Secret Agent* (1907), while *Under Western Eyes* (1911) is set among Russian revolutionaries. But it was not until the publication of *Chance* in 1913 that Conrad gained real success.

## THE NIGGER OF THE 'NARCISSUS'
### ◆ 1897 ◆

*Jimmy Wait, a black seaman from St Kitts (below),* and Donkin, a worthless cockney shirker, are just two of the crew aboard the *Narcissus* on its journey from India to London. Other vividly drawn characters are the fanatically religious Craik and the veteran sailor Singleton. Wait falls ill at the outset and Singleton predicts that he will die when land is sighted. The presence of the proud, withdrawn Wait exercises a subtly destructive influence, aggravated by bad weather, but eventually the Captain confronts the forces of disintegration.

William Westall: Gulf of Carpentian The Admiralty/E. T. Archive

## AN OUTCAST OF THE ISLANDS
### ◆ 1896 ◆

*'The mere scenery got a great hold on me* as I went on', Conrad wrote of this, his second novel. Following on from *Almayer's Folly,* it concerns the fate of Willems, a European man, abandoned by his own people to live out the rest of his days in virtual isolation on a remote Malayan island (above). Cut off from the locals and shunned by the few visiting white men, he is a perpetual outcast. The eerie stillness of the surroundings and shimmering half-light seem to reflect Willems' spiritual detachment; but then, unexpectedly, he falls in love. Aissa, a native girl, is the object of his affections, and is within his reach – for a price. He learns that he may have her if he sabotages the business of the English trader Almayer. This he accordingly does, but with unforeseen and tragic repercussions. Conrad wrote of Willems, 'Obviously I could not be indifferent to a man on whose head I had brought so much evil.'

H. N. O'Neil: A Volunteer (detail)/Fine Art Photographic Library

## HEART OF DARKNESS

**✦ 1902 ✦**

*A journey into the unexplored reaches of Africa* (above) moves the reader on two levels. It resembles Conrad's own experiences as a steamboat commander on the Upper Congo; and it symbolizes a journey into the darkness of the inner self, where civilized restraints are not acknowledged. The Conrad-like narrator is Marlow, already encountered in *Lord Jim*. Appointed to command a trading company's steamer, Marlow makes an interminable journey up an African river. He is soon sickened by the brutal exploitation of the Africans, and feels isolated among the petty-minded, materialistic traders and company men he meets. They all hate and fear a certain Kurtz, an outstandingly successful ivory trader operating further upriver. Marlow is strangely drawn to him, even when he realizes that Kurtz has in fact succumbed to the "darkness". He now tries to bring the sick Kurtz back to civilization.

## NOSTROMO

**✦ 1904 ✦**

*The novel is dominated by the San Tomé silver mine* (right), which corrupts or destroys all the leading characters. The hero of the piece is Nostromo, the Italian foreman of dockworkers in the imaginary Latin American republic of Costaguana. The Costaguanan dictator, Ribiera, rules with the support of the mine's owner, Charles Gould, until he is overthrown by General Montero, who whips up popular feeling against foreigners. Gould becomes obsessed with the idea of saving the mine's silver from being seized by the rebel forces, and enlists the help of Martin Decoud, a French journalist. Decoud and Nostromo sail off with a large consignment of silver, but collide with an enemy boat. Nostromo leaves Decoud and the silver on an uninhabited island and goes for help. Decoud, unhinged by the solitude of the island, commits suicide. The once-incorruptible Nostromo now surreptitiously begins making trips to the island to retrieve the 'lost' silver for his own use . . .

## THE SECRET AGENT
### ◆ 1907 ◆

*The serenity of Greenwich Park* (above) forms the backdrop for the novel's unexpected climax. A dingy little stationer's in Soho serves as a front for its owner, Adolf Verloc, an anarchist and an informer who works for both the British police and a foreign embassy. A crisis occurs when Verloc is summoned to the embassy and told that his pay will be cut off unless he manufactures a "senseless terrorist outrage" that will end British tolerance of the anarchists. Believing his simple-minded brother-in-law Stevie to be the perfect instrument, Verloc takes him to Greenwich Park with the intention in mind of blowing up the Observatory . . .

## UNDER WESTERN EYES
### ◆ 1911 ◆

*Set among Russian revolutionaries* (below) working to overthrow the Tsarist regime, the novel is full of intrigue. The chief character, Kirylo Razumov is a student whose quiet existence is disrupted when a fellow-student, Victor Haldin, takes refuge in his room. Haldin, who has just assassinated the Tsar's most vicious minister, appeals to him for help. Razumov agrees, but later loses his nerve and denounces his friend – a crime for which he eventually receives a curiously apt punishment.

## CHANCE
### ◆ 1913 ◆

*The troubled circumstances of Flora de Barral and her seafaring husband* (left) form the basis of this popular novel. Flora is a motherless young girl whose bankrupted father is suddenly imprisoned. The shock takes Flora close to suicide, but she is befriended by her former neighbours, the Fynes, and by Mrs Fyne's brother, Captain Roderick Anthony. Flora marries Anthony, and they live on board his ship, where they are later joined by Flora's father, now released from prison. But chance – and the machinations of the now resentful Mrs Fyne – keep husband and wife apart. Flora believes she is merely an object of pity to Anthony, while he supposes that she has married him purely as a form of refuge. De Barral, now wild with jealousy towards his son-in-law, resolves to poison Captain Anthony.

# THE RAPE OF AFRICA

**What Conrad witnessed in the Belgian Congo – the brutal handiwork of one greedy man – was only the "heart of darkness" beating within a continent similarly threatened from other quarters.**

In *Lord Jim*, Conrad writes of the early European traders who went to Borneo in search of pepper, seeing them as heroes suffering for a great cause:

*"desire made them defy death in a thousand shapes . . . It made them great! By Heavens! it made them heroic . . . they left their bones to lie bleaching on distant shores, so that wealth might flow to the living at home."*

Conrad was bewitched by the romance of adventure, and by dramatic settings where men worked out their moral destiny. But when this spirit of pioneering adventure was overtaken by rank imperialist exploitation, he loathed its brutalities. Even more, he loathed the hypocritical rhetoric that surrounded it.

Conrad spent four months in the Congo in 1890 at the helm of a river-steamer for a Belgian company, and he recorded the horror of what he saw there in *Heart of Darkness*, a savage condemnation of European imperialism at the turn of the century. The great 'scramble for Africa', which Conrad described as "the vilest scramble for loot that ever disfigured the history of human conscience", was completed in the astonishingly short space of 20 years. In 1879 only a small part of Africa was subject to foreign domination. By 1900 virtually the whole of that vast continent had been pillaged and appropriated by imperialist powers.

## ONE MAN'S WISH

This was not the work of the missionaries or the explorers, for they had neither territorial nor commerical interest in Africa. It was the combined work of European governments and businessmen who coveted Africa's rich resources. And in the beginning it was the work of one man alone – King Leopold II of Belgium. This ruler of a tiny, confined, European state, sought to satisfy his private greed and yearning for power overseas.

In 1876 Leopold founded, in Brussels, the International Association for the Exploration and Civilisation of Africa. He was its president and he took care to instruct the world in the nobility of his purpose: 'To open to civilisation the only part of the globe where it has not yet penetrated . . . to pierce the shadows which envelope whole peoples is, I dare to say, a crusade worthy of this century of progress.'

**Leopold II**
*Leopold Louis Philippe Marie Victor (right), King of the Belgians from 1865 to 1909, was a man of huge ambition and avarice. He set his sights on an overseas colony in which to expand his sphere of influence and personal profit. The Congo made easy pickings.*

Mary Evans Picture Library

**Henry Stanley**
*(left) Acclaimed throughout Europe for his recent explorations of the Congo Basin and his search for the source of the Nile, Stanley cut an heroic figure. He was ideal material to spearhead Leopold's venture into the Congo. His 'scientific stations' were set up with the enthusiastic support of the watching world – but once garrisoned, they were, in fact, armed outposts of empire.*

Mary Evans Picture Library

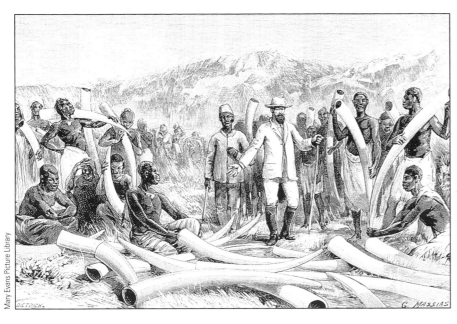

Henry Stanley, a lion among explorers, who had made a recent historic expedition from Zanzibar to the lower Congo, was appointed Leopold's chief agent. He was charged to create a chain of commercial and scientific stations across the heart of central Africa. He launched steamer routes, signed treaties with tribal chieftains and founded the stations. Each station had a garrison – ostensibly to protect its Christian missions and to lead an assault on Arab slavers, such as the loathsome Tipoo-Tib, who operated in the interior.

But Leopold had private ends in view. He gained control over the Congo and persuaded the European powers, by a clever manipulation of their diplomats, to recognize him as owner as well as ruler of the 'Congo Free State'. Better, he argued, to make the Congo an 'international area of free trade' than to let it fall into the hands of any one of the great powers. So Leopold became the owner of the largest private estate in history, an area almost the size of India and 77 times larger than Belgium. He financed the project almost entirely out of his own pocket.

***The booty***
*The true motives behind the colonization of the Congo were the ivory of elephant tusks (above), and rubber (above right). Every developed country was in the throes of industrialization and was therefore a ready marketplace for rubber – and ill-disposed to criticise Leopold's methods of obtaining it.*

The Congo was rich in ivory. It also had something of infinitely greater value to industrial Europe: forest upon forest of rubber trees. With his finances running low, Leopold came up with an easy solution to his shortage of capital. By a decree of 1885, he declared all 'vacant land' in the Congo to be his personal property. It was a simple matter after that to make the land vacant.

## HUMAN SACRIFICE
The lives of between five and eight million Congolese were sacrificed to Leopold's greed. He kept for himself the commercial exploitation of the now vacant lands, or granted it to concessionary companies which he nominated, and in many of which he had holdings. The state administrators and the company agents received premiums on the amount of rubber they collected. They were also instructed to exact taxation from the Congolese

***The excuse***
*The King's justification, in the eyes of the civilized world, was the abhorrent slave trade (left) which then blighted the lives of Congolese villagers. Arab slavers often exploited tribal rivalries and used one tribe to attack and capture others. Thorough publicity given to such horrors made Leopold's 'Christian' exploits seem a mission of mercy. His actions did much to suppress Arab slaving profits, but he too used black against black to murder and subjugate the population.*

73

Mary Evans Picture Library

who worked the forests for them, and since there was no currency, the taxes were levied in kind – in labour, or in flesh.

If an African worker disobeyed or displeased his master, or if he did not deliver his quota of rubber or ivory, it was commonplace for him to lose a hand. The masters were usually Africans them-selves, middlemen in a barbaric trade, who would demonstrate their zeal by presenting to their white bosses whole basketloads of hands. One state offi-cial told an American missionary in 1899 that every time a 'forest-guard' or Congolese soldier went out to collect rubber he was given cartridges and required to bring back every unused cartridge or, for every used one, a right hand. The same official claimed that in six months on the Mom-boyo river 6000 cartridges were used. An account from a state official in the Ubangi region details the 'efficiency' of the system:

'Method of procedure was to arrive in canoes at a village, the inhabitants of which invariably bolted on their arrival; the soldiers were then landed, and commenced looting, taking all the chickens, grain, etc., out of the houses; after this they attacked the natives until able to seize their women; these women were kept as hostages until the Chief of the district brought in the required number of kilogrammes of rubber. The rubber having been brought, the women were sold back to their owners for a couple of goats a-piece, and

**The Berlin Congress**
*(above) A summit meeting in 1884 to discuss the Congo was convinced by Leopold's arguments. They allowed him to take possession of the Congo rather than expose it to the opportunism of any one super-power.*

**Milking for rubber**
*All stages in the processing of rubber were labour intensive. But when the cost of labour was no more than violence and bullets, the profits to be made were massive.*

Mary Evans Picture Library

74

**Humanitarian champion**

*The British Consul to the Belgian Free State, Roger Casement (seated, left), appalled by what he saw, began to campaign against Belgian tyranny. After his posting ended, he compiled a report which swung public opinion. He was later hanged as a traitor for pursuing another cause dear to his heart – Irish republicanism.*

**Congo Railway Company**

*Leopold gave priority to better communications – to the steamship routes, road-building and, above all, the railway (right). The easy transportation of rubber, ivory and troops facilitated rapid, efficient exploitation of this vast, previously intractable region. To outside observers it seemed, of course, the right arm of civilization reaching deep into Africa's heathen heartlands.*

**Moneygrubber**

*When the King's true mercenary motives became clear, the Belgian parliament was shamed by the rest of Europe into taking the reins of power out of the monarch's hands and ousting his instruments of rule from the rubber plantations. Leopold held on grimly to his interests (left), some of which had buttressed his public image as a philanthropist. But before his death in 1909 he lost his 'private estate' in its entirety.*

so . . . from village to village until the requisite amount of rubber had been collected.'

An Englishman who worked on the Congo was sitting one evening at Bopoto, smoking with a Belgian official, Lieutenant Blochter. He recalled: 'It was late in the evening when suddenly a force of his [the Lieutenant's] troops returned from an expedition on which he had sent them in the morning. The sergeant held up triumphantly a number of ears fastened together on a string . . . The soldiers were praised for their success, and ordered to return next day and capture the chief.'

No matter how much rubber a worker, or a 'ganger', brought in, the only way that he could please his superiors was to bring in even more the next day. Atrocity heaped upon atrocity. The Congo Railway Company boasted that 'friends of humanity will find that the Congo railway is the means *par excellence* of allowing civilisation to penetrate rapidly and surely into the unknown depths of Africa'. But in *Heart of Darkness* the railway is seen for what it was – an instrument for hastening the mechanism of oppression.

In 1898 Roger Casement, an Irishman and a seasoned servant of the British Consular system, was

Mary Evans Picture Library

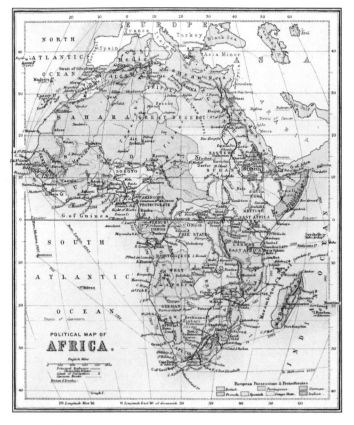

Royal Geographical Society

***Other kinds of hell***
*In* Lord Jim, *the vile Chester and Robinson contemplate the ultimate colonial project – guano mining (above), in which coolie labour was sweated to death in return for quick, vast profits. This was one of many new variations on a theme springing up worldwide.*

***Up for grabs***
*The rush to condemn Leopold was only surpassed by the rush to imitate him. The entire continent was quickly partitioned into European colonies (above). Rivalry for 'a place in the sun' is thought to have contributed to World War I – a conflict in which borders could be 'adjusted' and 'loot' redistributed among the competing plunderers.*

made British Consul for the Congo Free State. He was a fearless opponent of cruelty and exploitation and, between 1901 and 1903, he carried out a thorough investigation of the Congolese barbarities. (In his campaign for change, he tried to enlist the help of Conrad himself.) The report was published in February 1904 and shocked world opinion with the enormity of Leopold's crimes.

In England, E. D. Morel founded the Congo Reform Association to campaign against Leopold. Leopold himself established a commission of inquiry: it found that any miseries to which his African kingdom were subjected were the work of sleeping sickness and smallpox. But the impact of Casement's report forced a change. A more impartial Belgian commission supported Casement's findings and there was a change in the Congo government.

## THE CONGO ANNEXED

In return for massive loans of money in 1890 and 1895, Leopold had offered the Belgian government the right to annex the Congo state in 1901, should they wish to. They did not take up the option then, but in 1906, under the pressure of world opinion and their own unease, they voted to annex the Congo Free State. Leopold held out until 1908. He had ruled the Congo for 24 years as his personal commercial monopoly.

The King fought long and hard to retain a profitable source of income. He insisted that Belgium should guarantee the continuation of the *Fondation de la Couronne*, a corporation 'owning' one-tenth

of the country and whose revenue from rubber financed the King's acts of public beneficence. The *Fondation* survived for a year before public opinion put a stop to its operations.

During the first ten years of Belgian administration, free trade was wholly restored and the English reformers ceased to clamour for change. There were other areas of the world where other imperialist countries were invading, exploiting and oppressing. Casement, for instance, turned his attention to the atrocities white traders were committing along the Putumayo river in Peru.

## 'FREE-FOR-ALL'

Leopold's personal coup had long since whetted the appetites of other European governments. When, in 1888, Leopold said that 'the world ought to be our objective' and that 'there are no small nations, there are only small minds', he spoke the kind of rhetoric to fire the mind and heart of every imperialist. In just 18 months (1883-1885), South-West Africa, Togoland, the Cameroons and East Africa all came under German rule. Great Britain, France and Portugal followed Germany's example. By 1900, although Leopold of Belgium was a man disgraced, desperately clinging to his private fiefdom, the great carve-up of Africa was virtually complete.

Everywhere, whether in the Congo, or the East Indies or South America (where Conrad set *Nostromo*), the writer witnessed the same evil. His spokesman-narrator Marlow criticizes all men who would "tear treasure out of the bowels of the land . . . with no more moral purpose at the back of it than there is in burglars breaking into a safe". These were not adventurers:
*"They were conquerors, and for that you only want brute force – nothing to boast of . . . They grabbed what they could get for the sake of what was to be got. It was just robbery with violence, aggravated murder on a great scale, and men going at it blind – as is very proper for those who tackle a darkness. The conquest of the earth, which mostly means the taking it away from those who have a different complexion or slightly flatter noses than ourselves, is not a very pretty thing when you look into it too much."*

# E. M. FORSTER

## ◆ *1879-1970* ◆

'One of the most esteemed English novelists of his time',
Edward Morgan Forster was a shy, modest man. Brought up in
a suburban, middle-class household, dominated by his mother
and great-aunt, Forster moved on to the cloistered world of
Cambridge intellectuals, before a trip to Italy triggered his first
work of fiction. But it was India which inspired the masterpiece
that was to be his final novel. He spent the second half of his
long life as a critic and campaigner, dying at the age of 91.

# RELUCTANT OUTSIDER

**An isolated, lonely man, Forster yearned for love in his private life, but was never at ease with public acclaim. 'I don't like popularity,' he wrote. 'It seems so mad.'**

By the age of 31, and the publication of his fourth novel, *Howards End*, Edward Morgan Forster had established himself as one of the great novelists of his time. Yet he always remained a sensitive, timid and modest man for whom friendship and the life of the imagination were more important than fame.

He was born in London on 1 January 1879. His mother, Lily, had been adopted as a child by Marianne Thornton into a wealthy merchant and banking family. Marianne, or 'Monie' as she was called, had encouraged Lily to marry her favourite nephew, Edward Forster, who had taken up architecture after graduating from Cambridge. He was 29 when he married Lily, but just three-and-a-half years later he was dead from consumption, leaving behind a son who was not yet two years old.

## IDYLLIC YEARS

Lily moved to a house in Stevenage, Hertfordshire, called Rooksnest. She thought the country air would be good for young Morgan's health, about which she was so obsessive that he was to reach middle age thinking of himself, quite wrongly, as frail. Rooksnest was a large house, complete with tennis court, paddock and orchard. At times Lily found it lonely there, but she and her son soon developed a deep and abiding love for the place.

There were frequent visits to Monie's home in Clapham where little Morgan was the admired and pampered darling of all the women. Talented and precocious, he discovered he could read to himself at the age of four and soon set out to improve the minds of the garden boys whom he befriended in his early years.

What he came to regard as his idyllic years at Rooksnest were spoiled when, at the age of 11, he was sent to Kent House Preparatory School in Eastbourne. The other boys jeered at him, calling him 'Mousie', and he became deeply unhappy. Life did not improve when, at the age of 14, the owner of Rooksnest refused to renew the lease and he and his mother moved to Tonbridge. Here he enrolled as a day-boy at the minor public school and acquired his life-long hatred of the public school system. A fellow pupil remembered him in the 1950s with the following words: 'Forster? . . . A little cissy. We took it out of him, I can tell you.'

At 18, Morgan went to King's College, Cambridge to read Classics and then History. Here he at last came into his own and developed a circle of friends, among them H. O. Meredith, an extremely clever man whom Forster was to later describe as 'my first great love'.

Meredith introduced Forster to the Apostles, the most exclusive intellectual society in Cambridge, which later became the nucleus of the Bloomsbury Group. Its members included Bertrand Russell, John Maynard Keynes, Lytton Strachey, Roger

## Key Dates

**1879** born in London

**1880** father dies

**1893** sent to Tonbridge School

**1897** becomes student at Cambridge

**1901** first trip to Italy

**1905** *Where Angels Fear to Tread* published

**1906** meets Syed Ross Masood

**1910** *Howards End* published; acclaimed as great novelist

**1912-13** visits India

**1915-19** working in Alexandria

**1921** second visit to India

**1924** *A Passage to India* published

**1930** meets Bob Buckingham

**1945** mother dies

**1946** moves to Cambridge

**1969** awarded Order of Merit

**1970** dies in Coventry

**Remote father**
*(left) Edward Forster died before his son reached his second birthday. 'I have never seen myself in him', wrote Forster, 'and letters from him and the photographs have not helped.'*

**Adoring mother**
*Forster and his mother (seen together right) enjoyed an extraordinarily close relationship. In later life, he wrote that although she could be 'intermittently tiresome', she provided him with 'a sort of rich subsoil where I have been able to rest and grow'.*

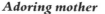

By permission of the Provost and Scholars of King's College, Cambridge

By permission of the Provost and Scholars of King's College, Cambridge

Fry, Goldsworthy Lowes Dickinson and Leonard Woolf. They openly attacked the values which Forster had learned to hate at Tonbridge – the snobbery and oppression of English provincial life – and discussed freely and easily such subjects as religion, sex and homosexuality.

This circle regarded Lytton Strachey's nickname for Forster, 'the Taupe', as apt, because 'of his faint physical resemblance to a mole, but principally because he seemed intellectually and emotionally to travel unseen underground and every now and again pop up unexpectedly with some subtle observation or delicate quip which somehow or other

he had found in the depths of the earth or of his own soul'.

Forster was probably well aware by now that he was emotionally and sexually drawn to men. But, with his prim upbringing and in the wake of the Oscar Wilde scandal, he tried to contain his dark secret. It was impossible to admit to his friends that he might be homosexual, let alone imagine having physical relations with them.

Forster left Cambridge in 1901 with no definite plans for the future, except for a general hope that he could establish himself as a journalist or writer of fiction. A legacy from Monie had financed

### King's College

(above) *Forster enjoyed himself immensely at King's College, Cambridge. If he had been 'immature, uninteresting and unphilosophic' before he went up to King's, once there he spread his wings under the liberating influence of 'the Apostles' and others.*

### Childhood paradise

(right) *Forster drew this map of Rooksnest, the house he called 'my childhood and safety'. With its pond, mysterious attics and neighbouring meadow, Rooksnest was an earthly paradise for a young child. Howards End, the house in the novel of that name, is a lovingly recreated picture of this childhood home. It shares with Rooksnest the magnificent wych-elm 'leaning a little over the house'.*

revelation of the 'greatness' present in the world.

In 1903 Forster, along with other ex-Apostles, began to contribute to *The Independent Review*, a Liberal periodical founded to argue against Tory imperialism, and advocate social reform. The following year, having moved into a flat with his mother, Forster began a series of lectures on Italian art and history. He was kept busy, teaching and writing, and he had the ever-loving, perhaps over-loving, support of his mother. But these were lonely times for him. His friendship with Meredith had ended, and at 25 Forster felt that his life was 'straightening into something rather sad and dull'.

## LIBERATING INFLUENCE

A chance of a change came when he took up an appointment in Germany as tutor to the three eldest daughters of Countess von Arnim. At first the Countess – better known as the novelist 'Elizabeth' of the best-seller *Elizabeth and her German Garden* – tried to bully and patronize Forster. But she began to realize that he was not the mousy, undistinguished person she had thought he was. And reading one of his articles in *The Independent Review* confirmed her new opinion. From that point the two got on very well and Forster enjoyed his months in Germany.

He returned to England in time for the publication of *Where Angels Fear to Tread* in October 1905, and it was not long before he met a young, handsome Indian, Syed Ross Masood, who was to become in his own way an extraordinary, liberating, influence for Forster.

Forster had been asked to tutor Masood in Latin

***Italian inspiration***
*(above) 'Charming' San Gimignano, which Forster visited on his first trip to Italy, was the model for Monteriano in* Where Angels Fear to Tread.

***The Bloomsbury Group***
*Forster had close contacts with the Bloomsbury Group, the intellectual circle that included Virginia Woolf (centre) and her husband Leonard (right, with pipe).*

his education and it now paid for his first trip to Italy, on which he was accompanied by his mother.

It was on the route south, travelling down to Naples and Sicily, that he finally wrote his first successful piece of fiction, a fantasy called *The Story of a Panic*. In writing it he trusted his imagination for the first time and became confident that he was indeed a writer. Forster and his mother had been strictly tourists – 'It was a very timid outing', he said. But the months he spent in Italy had liberated him, and helped him to find his writer's voice.

On returning to England, mother and son moved into a hotel in Bloomsbury so as to be close to the Working Men's College where Forster was to teach Latin once a week. His old friend H. O. Meredith lived nearby and the two re-established a friendship of growing affection and intimacy. For Forster, it was of immense importance – a

ALEXANDRIE. PLACE DES CONSULS COTÉ EST

*By permission of the Provost and Scholars of King's College, Cambridge*

***In Egypt . . .***
*(above) In the liberal atmosphere of Alexandria, where he worked during World War I, Forster at last found love – with a young Egyptian, Mohammed el Adl.*

***. . . and India***
*Forster's first trip to India in 1912-13 took in Delhi (below), where he and his friend Masood were obliged to entertain constant streams of visitors.*

*Walter Crane: The Chandni Chowk, Delhi, evening after rain/Fine Art Photographic Library*

to prepare his entry to Oxford. He was immediately captivated by his pupil's warmth, spontaneity and effusiveness. Masood was well over six foot tall, and if a lesson bored him, he might pick Forster up bodily and tickle him. The novelist was jolted out of his Englishness, surprised and delighted by Masood's extravagances. Little by little he grew to love him, and though the sexual love was not reciprocated, a bond of genuine friendship developed between the two men.

## LITERARY ACCLAIM

In 1908 *A Room With a View* was published and two years later came *Howards End*. His mother was shocked by it, but the press hailed it as the season's great novel, and the shy, reclusive Forster became a reluctant celebrity. As he wrote to Dickinson, 'I don't like popularity. It seems so mad . . . I go about saying I like the money because one is simply bound to be pleased about something on such an occasion. But I don't even like that very much . . . No, It is all insanity.'

He continued his writings, but longed to see Masood, who had recently returned to his home in Aligarh, northern India. In 1912 Forster decided to make his first visit to India. He spent two delightful weeks with Masood, first in Aligarh and then in nearby Delhi, before moving on to Lahore. There he stayed with Malcolm Darling, a former fellow-student at King's, and his wife. Lahore was Anglo-Indian land, and Forster hated it. Although the Darlings were liberal in their attitude to Indians, others were less so. It was here that Forster met the petty-minded 'Turtons and Burtons', whom he was to write about in *A Passage to India*.

Through the Darlings, Forster became the guest and friend of the 24-year-old Maharajah of Dewas State Senior. The Maharajah had a 'clever merry little face in a huge turban', and Forster liked him immediately. The two men met up again later in Delhi, and forged a friendship which was second only to Forster's friendship with Masood.

Eventually it was time to return to England, and Forster made his way back to Weybridge. It was a happy homecoming, and he felt matured and broadened by his experiences. He made several

## SYED ROSS MASOOD

Forster dedicated *A Passage to India* to Syed Ross Masood. They met in 1906 and were friends for life. Masood was a striking figure, self-confident, flamboyant and extremely affectionate to all his friends. In Forster's words, he regarded the world 'as a room full of secondary persons with himself feeling intensely in the centre' He is one of Forster's models for Aziz – just as Fielding shows many of Forster's qualities.

The grandson of the famous Muslim reformer, Sir Syed Ahmed Khan, Masood was a fervent Muslim patriot who loved to tell stories of how he had succeeded in putting down members of the British Raj. But during his years in England he acquired a large circle of English friends and after leaving Oxford he returned to India with much reluctance.

Here he married in 1915 and was given an administrative post by the Nizam of Hyderabad. Following the collapse of his marriage, and then of his finances in the world stock market crash of 1929, he took the post of Vice-Chancellor of the Anglo-Oriental College. Out-manoeuvred by his enemies, he felt forced to resign, a blow from which he never fully recovered. He died from kidney disease in 1937, aged 47.

In Forster's obituary tribute to Masood, he wrote: 'My own debt to him is incalculable. He woke me up out of my suburban and academic life, showed me new horizons and a new civilization . . . Until I met him, India was a vague jumble of rajahs, sahibs, babus and elephants . . .'

pilgrimages to the author Edward Carpenter at the house he shared in Millthorpe in Derbyshire with his working-class lover George Merrill. On one such visit Merrill touched Forster on the backside. It was a casual gesture but remained with Forster for years. 'The sensation was unusual, and I still remember it, as I remember the position of the long vanished tooth . . . It seemed to go straight through the small of my back into my ideas, without involving my thoughts.' Apparently the entire plot of *Maurice*, his novel about homosexual love, rushed into his mind.

With the outbreak of World War I, Forster became depressed and unsettled. He was a pacifist by nature, but wanted to participate at some level. In November 1915 he accordingly left for Alexandria in Egypt, where he was to work as a 'searcher' for the International Red Cross. His duties were not very onerous – they involved gathering information from the wounded in hospital about fellow-soldiers reported missing – and he had plenty of time for his writing.

**Lifelong friendships**
*Forster was devoted to his friends. Above, he is pictured flanked by Bob Buckingham and J. R. Ackerley. Below is his friend and confidante Florence Barger – 'She loves me and I her,' he said.*

## LOVE AT LAST

In some ways Alexandria suited Forster perfectly. It had a cosmopolitan community of homosexuals and in 1916 he finally 'parted with respectability', embarking on a number of experimental relationships until, in 1917, he fell in love. The recipient of his love was an Egyptian tram conductor called Mohammed el Adl. They made cautious overtures to each other, amused rather than apalled by their different backgrounds, and after a time spent nights as well as days together. For Forster it was joyous. He told a friend, Florence Barger, 'It is awful to think of the thousands who go through youth without ever knowing. I have known in a way before, but never like this. My luck has been amazing.' His 'luck' held for several years, surviving even Mohammed's marriage.

By the end of October 1918, Turkey had surrendered and Forster's work for the Red Cross came to an end. Returning to England in 1919, he worked briefly as literary editor of the Socialist *Daily Herald* and wrote articles and reviews for a variety of periodicals. He also worked on the novel which was to become *A Passage to India*, and when his old friend, the Maharajah of Dewas State

**Relaxing in India**
*(below) Forster is shown in 1921, playing cards with the Maharajah of Dewas State Senior and his retinue.*

Senior, invited him to return to India as private secretary, he accepted gladly.

Increasingly, however, Forster felt that it was not of 'any use to go on muddling with work that gave me no satisfaction, and was of no essential importance', so when the opportunity arose for him to extend his stay in Dewas, he did not take it. He hated leaving the Maharajah, whom he described as 'one of the sweetest and saintliest men I have ever known', but it was with relief that he left the confusion of Dewas to stay with Masood.

On returning to England in 1922 he started a correspondence with J. R. Ackerley, a then unknown writer. Forster praised his work, Ackerley was flattered and the two became fast friends. Although never lovers, they saw each other regularly, and it was through Ackerley that the 51-year-old Forster met a 26-year-old policeman, Bob Buckingham, in 1930. Buckingham was warm-hearted, genial and eager to better himself. Forster gladly took on his literary education, deriving as much pleasure from the enterprise as did Buckingham. The two men embarked on a relationship which brought Forster great happiness. As he wrote in 1932: 'I have been happy for two years. It mayn't be over yet, but I want to write it down before it gets spoiled by the pain.'

Their close friendship could have been jeopardized by Buckingham's marriage to May Hockey, but May, too, became a valued friend. And Forster even became godfather to their son, whom they named Robert Morgan in his honour. Forster was deeply moved, and through the years he helped with Rob's education and enjoyed being part of the Buckingham family. When Rob died tragically at the age of 29, Forster grieved as though for his own son and provided Rob's young wife and children with a regular allowance.

In 1925 Forster and his mother moved into the only existing house designed by his father – West Hackhurst in Abinger Hammer, near Dorking.

**Krishna**
*The Hindu god (shown in blue) 'sports with the cowherds'.*

British Library

# THE FESTIVAL OF GOKUL ASHTAMI

The last section of *A Passage to India* centres on a festival celebrating the birth of Krishna. According to Forster 'The Krishna festival [in the novel] closely follows the great celebration of Gokul Ashtami, which I attended for nine days in the palace of Dewas State Senior, and which was the strangest and strongest Indian experience ever granted me.' The Festival honours the god Krishna, supposedly born at Gokul, and its aim was to achieve *bhakti* or direct union with the Divine through love.

Much of the ritual had been invented by the Maharajah of Dewas. At its centre was the continual singing of hymns around the altar in the Old Palace, to the accompaniment of cymbals and a harmonium. The festival ended with the announcement of Krishna's birth and a procession from the Old Palace to the Tank, where a clay model of the village of Gokul was ceremoniously thrown into the waters.

---

Life here went on with a Victorian formality which Forster escaped on visits to the London flat he now maintained for his private life.

Throughout the 1920s and '30s he wrote essays and articles on a wide range of subjects, many of which reflected his devotion to the cause of free speech and his hatred of Nazism and Stalinism. His principles were very much those of the newly founded National Council for Civil Liberties and, in 1934, he agreed to become its first president.

By the time World War II broke out, Lily was crippled by rheumatism and was very demanding. When she died in 1945, at the age of 90, Forster felt drowned by waves of despair and imagined that it would not be long before he died too.

## FINAL HONOURS

He made one last trip to India after which he was elected an Honorary Fellow of King's College, with the offer, which he accepted, of a room in college and living quarters nearby. Towards the end of his life Forster reflected, 'Being an important person is a full time job and is bound to generate some inward futility and pretentiousness . . . You need not do any thing – you've arrived . . . And I don't.' But he was far from idle. In his seventies he visited the United States, worked with Eric Crozier on the libretto for Benjamin Britten's opera *Billy Budd*, and wrote two books, one being a biography of his great-aunt and benefactor Marianne Thornton. He continued to write articles until well into his eighties.

In 1953 he was made a Companion of Honour and, in 1969, at the age of 90, received, the Order of Merit. The following year, at the age of 91, he suffered what was to be a final stroke, and on 7 June he died in the Coventry home of his beloved friends Bob and May Buckingham, holding May's hand. His ashes were scattered in their garden, and five years later, when Bob Buckingham died, his too were scattered over the same rose-bush.

**Order of Merit**
*(right) In the New Year's Honours List of 1969 Forster was awarded the Order of Merit, one of Britain's most prestigious decorations. King's College organized a luncheon in dual celebration of this and his 90th birthday.*

Spink and Son Ltd

**Grand old man**
*(below) Forster stands in his bedroom at King's, where he was made an Honorary Fellow in 1945 – and lionized as 'the greatest living Kingsman'. He suffered his final, fatal stroke there – but Bob Buckingham took him home to Coventry to die.*

Study by Cecil Beaton/Camera Press, London

# A PASSAGE TO INDIA

**In Forster's final novel, the possibility of friendship across the barriers of race and culture is shattered when a young Indian doctor is accused of assaulting an English woman.**

Forster's *A Passage to India* is recognized as a masterpiece of 20th-century fiction. A contemporary novelist and critic described it as 'more than a study of racial contrasts and disabilities. It is intensely personal and . . . intensely cosmic'. On one level, Forster has written a social and political satire on the effect of British rule in India. But he has also written a novel which minutely examines and evokes the relationships between people, places and the spiritual forces that govern human behaviour and understanding.

## GUIDE TO THE PLOT

Aziz, a Moslem (Muslim) doctor practising in the city of Chandrapore, meets an ageing English woman in a moonlit mosque one night. It is a strange and significant encounter. Aziz has just been discussing the impossibility of friendship with the English, but somehow Mrs Moore, newly arrived in India, appears to be a kindred spirit and seems to understand him completely. "You are an Oriental," he tells her. They leave the mosque together. She returns to the Club, which he, as an Indian, is not allowed to enter. He returns home, his heart lifted by the meeting, feeling that he seemed to "own the land as much as anyone owned it".

Mrs Moore is the mother of Ronny Heaslop, the young City Magistrate (called "Red-nose" by Aziz's friends). She has come to India with Adela Quested, an earnest, honest, rather unattractive young woman who is deliberating over whether to marry Ronny. Adela longs to see what she calls "the real India". Mr Fielding, principal of the local college, tells her to "Try seeing Indians".

***Sporting equals***
*A sudden, short-lived relationship of mutual respect between Indian and Englishman occurs when Aziz and a "stray subaltern" share an impromptu game of polo. "'If only they were all like that,' each thought."*

The Collector, head of the British civil administration, holds an unheard of 'Bridge Party' to which he invites the important English, Moslems and Hindus of the district. This official attempt to bridge the gulf between the races is a ridiculous failure; most of the British guests consider it beneath their dignity to socialize with the "natives".

Mrs Moore and Adela do get their chance to have an informal social meeting with Indians when Fielding invites them to tea, along with Aziz and Professor Godbole, the enigmatic Brahman (priestly-caste Hindu). This second attempt at a union is more successful than the Bridge Party. But the good feelings are spoilt when Ronny Heaslop arrives to take his mother and Adela to a polo match: "He did not mean to be rude to the two men [Aziz and Godbole], but the only link he could be conscious of with an Indian was the official, and neither happened to be his subordinate. As private individuals he forgot them."

The party breaks up, but before they separate Professor Godbole sings a song to the god Krishna. He sings "Come, come, come, come, come." But – he tells the women – the god "neglects to come".

Anxious to show hospitality to the two English women, Aziz has invited the group from the tea party to visit the "extraordinary" Marabar Caves, in the hills that can be seen some distance from Chandrapore. He goes to an inordinate amount of trouble and expense, but the expedition gets off to a bad start when Fielding and Godbole miss the train (because Godbole has misjudged the length of a prayer).

Mrs Moore visits only one of the caves,

### Divided city

*The novel begins with a description of Chandrapore, contrasting the sprawling Indian settlement beside a rubbish-strewn section of the Ganges, with the sterile, "sensibly-planned" British Civil Station. These two elements of the city share "nothing . . . except the overarching sky".*

and finds it a terrifyingly claustrophobic experience. She hears a devastating "bou-oum" which reduces everything to the same meaningless echo. The echo seems to "undermine her hold on life". She sits and rests while Aziz and Adela explore further, gradually giving herself up to numbing despair.

After an awkward conversation about marriage, Aziz and Adela become separated near the mouths of a group of caves, and Adela takes a lift back to town. The rest of the party return to Chandrapore together. On their arrival, Aziz is arrested. Adela claims that he assaulted her in the Caves.

> *"We're not out here for the purpose of behaving pleasantly…We're out here to do justice and keep the peace…"*
>
> *"Your sentiments are those of a god," she said quietly…*
>
> *"India likes gods."…*
>
> *"And Englishmen like posing as gods."*

The arrest of Aziz polarizes the British and the Indians. The British herd together in their Club. "Pity, wrath, heroism, filled them", and they are eager for indiscriminate revenge on the "natives": "Call in the troops and clear the bazaars."

Fielding's support of Aziz makes him an outcast from the British community. Mrs Moore has become detached, irritable and uninterested. But her casual assertion that Aziz is innocent is enough to sow

seeds of doubt in Adela's mind – and enough to make Ronny decide to send her back to England.

The third section of the novel takes place two years later. Aziz is convinced that Fielding has betrayed him to marry Adela, and is so sickened by the English that he has left Chandrapore and – despite being a Moslem – has gone to work in the Hindu state of Mau, where Professor Godbole is Minister of Education. When Fielding makes an official visit, Aziz intends to ignore him. But against a backdrop of a strange, beautiful Hindu festival celebrat-

### Mosque

*(below) Resting in a beautiful mosque, symbolic centre of his Islamic religion, Aziz meets Mrs. Moore. He is a young Indian Moslem, she an old Englishwoman and a Christian – yet the two strike an instant and lasting spiritual bond.*

*In the Background*

## THE HINDU CASTE SYSTEM

Professor Godbole is a member of the highest caste in the Hindu hierarchy.

Hindu society was traditionally divided into four castes: first the Brahmans or priests, second the Kshatriyas or warriors, third the Vaisyas or farmers and traders, and fourth the Sudras who were the peasant and menial caste. Outside these fall the Penchama or outcastes, known as the untouchables. Over the centuries many subdivisions have arisen, so that now there are some 3,000 castes in India with over 25,000 sub-castes.

The caste system governs every aspect of Hindu life. Each caste forms a closed system within itself, contact with any outsider often being regarded as contaminating. When Godbole almost collides with the Moslem Aziz at the Krishna festival, he says "'Ah, you might make me late' – meaning that the touch of a non-Hindu would necessitate another bath . . ."

ing the birth of Krishna, there seems to be a possibility of reconciliation.

## A SPIRITUAL PASSAGE

Forster took the title of his novel from Walt Whitman's poem entitled 'Passage to India', which concerns the journey of the soul to the 'seas of god'. The English characters in the novel have, of course, made their physical 'passage to India'. But Forster is concerned with the emotional and spiritual journey of all the characters.

Forster later wrote that he wished that a novel was not something that just 'tells a story', but that it could be 'a melody, or perception of truth'. In *A Passage to India*, he had achieved this. The novel does tell a story. But it revolves around a single, ambiguous incident – the alleged assault in the Marabar Caves. It is never clear what actually happened in the Caves, and the real 'message', the 'perception of truth' in the novel, is more subtle and elusive than the events it describes.

At first, in the section called 'Mosque', there seems to be a chance of 'connection'

> *"Perhaps life is a mystery, not a muddle; they could not tell. Perhaps the hundred Indias which fuss and squabble so tiresomely are one, and the universe they mirror is one. They had not the apparatus for judging."*

across racial and religious barriers, and a possibility of being 'one with the universe' which Mrs Moore perceives. In 'Caves', all these hopes are shattered; the races divide, spiritual harmony is destroyed. Then in 'Temple' there is once again hope of universal love and friendship.

In the three sections of the novel, the mood and action changes with the setting, and India passes through the cycle of its seasons, from the cold to the hot to the rainy season – symbol of Hope and regeneration. Forster's sense of pattern and rhythm pervades the novel, preparing the reader for things to come, echoing past events, and giving a mystical significance to tiny details.

In the early chapters, Mrs Moore encounters a little wasp, and extends her Christian love to it:

*Going to hang up her cloak, she found that the tip of the peg was occupied by a small wasp . . . 'Pretty dear,' said Mrs Moore to the wasp. He did not wake, but her voice floated out, to swell the night's uneasiness.*

Ann and Bury Peerless

This simple, private example of Mrs Moore's 'universal love' is recalled in a vision in the final section of the book. During the Krishna festival, the image of Mrs Moore and a wasp on a stone appears to Godbole while he is in a trance-like state. He embraces them both in his sense of universal love and invites god to "Come, come, come, come."

## STRUGGLE AND SILENCE

The characters who are most 'successful' in terms of understanding and accepting the mystery of experience and the shapelessness that is India (and, by extension, the universe), are those who are able to remain silent. Godbole's refusal to explain the importance of the caves, and his strange lack of interest in the catastrophe surrounding Aziz gradually begins to make more sense. His aloofness is his wisdom, and at the end of the story he is a holy man, in the presence of God in the Temple, while the others still struggle and search for answers that they will probably never find.

with Indians: "The world, he believed, is a globe of men who are trying to reach one another". He warms to the boastful, warm-hearted doctor, for like Aziz, "he had dulled his craving for verbal truth and cared chiefly for truth of mood."

Their friendship is passionate and stimulating. Fielding risks his job and way of life in India to protest Aziz's innocence, yet they drift apart, with Aziz preferring to believe gossip rather than trust his friend's integrity. When they meet again, Aziz declares himself fiercely anti-British. Fielding has become more conservative since his marriage and wonders, "Would he today defy all his own people for the sake of a stray Indian?"

As they enjoy one last ride together, Aziz cries: ". . . we shall drive every blasted Englishman into the sea, and then . . . you and I shall be friends." Fielding exclaims: "Why can't we be friends now?", but their human voices and desires are no match for the forces that are destined to keep them apart . . . "'No, not yet,' . . . 'No, not there.'"

***The trip to the Caves***
*In an impulsive gesture of hospitality, Aziz takes Mrs. Moore and Adela to visit the Marabar Caves. The "untidy" landscape (above) is quite unlike the "romantic yet manageable" Lakes back in England. Aziz goes to great trouble, and even provides an elephant: "'Oh, what a surprise!' called the ladies politely. Aziz said nothing, but he nearly burst with pride and relief."*

Mrs Moore's intuitive and spiritual approach to her time in Chandrapore makes her in the end an indestructible part of India. She has little to say, but her influence is enormous. During the trial of Aziz her name is taken up and chanted in the streets by the crowds outside the courtroom. "Esmiss Esmoor" becomes one of the book's resounding echoes as she is claimed by the Indians as a saviour, and shrines are erected to her memory. By contrast, Adela is unable to let things be. Searching restlessly for more experience to understand India, she triggers disaster and alienation.

## FRIENDSHIP

The relationship between Aziz and Fielding is central to the novel. Aziz is anxious to believe that racial differences can be overcome, and Fielding sees no reason why he should not be friends

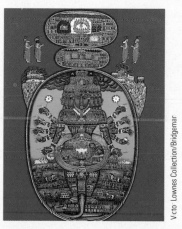

***Social outcast***
*After being the focus of British "fine emotion", Adela (right) becomes an outcast.*

***Universal love***
*In the novel's final section, Godbole aims to achieve divine union with Krishna (left) through love.*

87

# CHARACTERS IN FOCUS

The characters in *A Passage to India*, in their various social, ethnic and religious groups, move uneasily about each other, forming fragile connections which disintegrate under the burning Indian sky. Some characters, such as the bigoted Anglo-Indians, are almost caricatures (albeit accurate ones). Others, especially Aziz and Fielding, are developed much more deeply. English, Indian, Moslem, Christian, Hindu, rulers and ruled alike, struggle to achieve an intimacy that seems impossible.

## WHO'S WHO

**Dr Aziz**   An Indian doctor, educated in Western science, but whose heart is attuned to India and Islam.

**Mr Fielding**   An English teacher. The 'odd-man-out' at the Club, he rejects the notion of racial superiority.

**Mrs Moore**   An ageing Englishwoman, whose spiritual awareness has significant effects on those around her.

**Ronny Heaslop**   Mrs Moore's son. The City Magistrate.

**Adela Quested**   An honest, "cautious" woman who has come to India to decide whether to marry Ronny.

**Professor Godbole**   An enigmatic Brahman professor, who seems to speak in riddles.

**Major Callendar**   Aziz's boss at the hospital. "He longed for the good old days when an Englishman could satisfy his honour and no questions asked . . ."

**Hamindullah**   "The leading barrister of Chandrapore, with . . . dignified manner and Cambridge degree . . ." A close friend of Aziz.

**The Nawab Bahadur**   "A big proprietor and philanthropist", he finances Aziz's defence.

**Miss Derek**   British companion to a Maharani (princess).

**The Turtons**   The Collector (head of the civil administration) and his 'memsahib': "little gods" at Chandrapore.

*Adela Quested (left) is a "queer, cautious girl"* who has come to India to make her decision about whether to marry Ronny Heaslop, the City Magistrate in Chandrapore. However hard she tries, Adela never manages to fit in. She shocks Aziz with her inadvertently impertinent questioning about the number of wives he has. And at the Club her well-meaning attitude towards Indians make her "not pukka". "She was such a dry, sensible girl, and quite without malice: the last person in Chandrapore wrongfully to accuse an Indian." But she does . . .

Roger Coleman

*"A hard-bitten, good-tempered, intelligent fellow on the verge of middle age, with a belief in education", Fielding* (right) is an outsider in the British community of Chandrapore: "He had no racial feeling . . . the remark that did him most harm at the Club was a silly aside to the effect that the so-called white races are really pinko-gray." But he really goes beyond the pale when he protests Aziz's innocence, and so takes sides with an Indian: "He regretted taking sides. To slink through India unlabelled was his aim. Henceforward he would be called 'anti-British'."

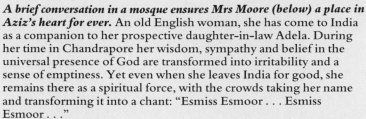

*A brief conversation in a mosque ensures Mrs Moore (below) a place in Aziz's heart for ever.* An old English woman, she has come to India as a companion to her prospective daughter-in-law Adela. During her time in Chandrapore her wisdom, sympathy and belief in the universal presence of God are transformed into irritability and a sense of emptiness. Yet even when she leaves India for good, she remains there as a spiritual force, with the crowds taking her name and transforming it into a chant: "Esmiss Esmoor . . . Esmiss Esmoor . . ."

*"An athletic little man," Aziz* (above) is a skilled doctor working as an assistant for the bigoted Civil Surgeon. He is an emotional and impulsive character, whose heart is steeped in Islam, in which he finds "an attitude towards life both exquisite and durable". Until his arrest he is eager to make friendships across the race barrier – afterwards he becomes fiercely anti-British.

*A priestly caste Hindu, Professor Godbole (left) has a detached, philosophical approach to "the muddle that is India",* which allows him to transcend the traumas that the other characters experience: "no eye could see what lay at the bottom of the Brahman's mind, and yet he had a mind and a heart too, and all his friends trusted him, without knowing why."

# 'ONLY CONNECT . . .'

**In his novels and other literary works, Forster upheld the cause of personal freedom. His inspiration was "the prose and the passion" of life – and the need to draw them together.**

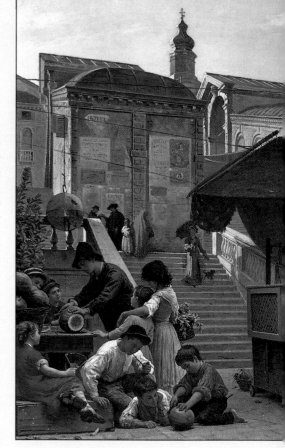

'I am quite sure I am not a great novelist', declared E. M. Forster in old age. But by now, more than 60 years after the publication of his last full-length work of fiction, this typically disconcerting remark looks like one of Forster's most serious misjudgements. He is a popular writer as well as a deeply serious one, intensely readable and yet so complex and subtle that his work can be enjoyed on any one of several levels.

An all-pervading concern in Forster's novels is with the stifling pressure society exerts on the individual. From first to last, Forster is hostile to the narrow-minded, self-righteous regime of 'Sawston', which appears in various guises throughout his novels. In *The Longest Journey*, Sawston is the oppressive, overbearing public school, while in *Where Angels Fear to Tread* it is embodied in the smugly confident provincial circle. Sawston cramps people's lives and prevents the expression of their true natures. Only a lucky few escape, like Lucy Honeychurch in *A Room with a View*, or Maurice, who becomes an 'outlaw' because of his sexual nature. Outside England, British India is, in Forster's eyes, Sawston supreme, adding to the barrier between classes a barrier between races that makes impossible any authentic connection between Englishman and Indian.

## BRIDGING THE GAP

'Connection' is Forster's highest value. For him, personal relationships are sacred – a conviction that gave rise to his notorious statement, 'If I had to choose between betraying my country and betraying my friend, I hope I should have the guts to betray my country.'

This does not mean that Forster regards

***Recurring symbols***
*(left and above) The indoors frequently symbolizes repression in Forster's work – while sunshine and the outdoor life imply freedom and vitality.*

the cultivated and 'caring' as superior people. It is one of his great strengths as a novelist that he recognizes qualities and defects in all groups. The cultured (for example, Cecil Vyse in *A Room with a View*) can be as shallow in their own way as the inhabitants of Sawston or the Wilcoxes of *Howards End*. And as Margaret Schlegel comes to recognize, her cultivation of personal relations is only possible because the Wilcoxes exist: "More and more do I refuse to draw my income and sneer at those who guarantee it." She hopes to bridge the gap between the Schlegels and the Wilcoxes: "Only connect the prose and the passion, and both will be exalted, and human love will be seen at its height."

As if to drive the message home, Forster also put the words "Only connect . . ." at the front of the novel, as an epigraph. Of *Howards End*, and also of his homosexual novel, *Maurice*, he wrote 'My defence at any Last Judgement would be "I was trying to connect up and use all the fragments I was born with."'

Paul Fischer: The Drawing Room/Fine Art Photographic Library

Antonio Paoletti: The Flower Stall/Fine Art Photographic Library

conscious one is of these things; how one flounders about.'

To take only a single example, Forster tends to identify life indoors with convention and constraint, whereas the outdoors stands for freedom and passion. *A Room with a View* is the story of how the 'view', or outdoors, triumphs over the 'room' – an act of liberation accomplished by the Emersons, beginning with their insistence that Lucy shall not go without a view in the Italian boarding house where they are all staying. The symbolism recurs in *Maurice*, where the hero reflects dismally that "Indoors was his place and there he'd moulder, a respectable pillar of society who has never had the chance to misbehave."

In *A Passage to India* the patterning – whether the appearances of a wasp or the symbolic roles of earth and sky – is still more complex, though the novel can be enjoyed without paying any conscious attention to it.

Even now, nobody knows why Forster stopped writing novels when he was still only in his forties. He himself gave various explanations – that he just 'drifted out of it', that he had 'nothing more to say' and, later on, that England had changed so completely that he no longer felt that he

knew anything at all about the place.

One of his earliest creative works, *The Story of a Panic,* was literally, inspired. In 1902, walking near Ravello in southern Italy, 'I sat down in a valley, a few miles above the town, and suddenly the first chapter of the story rushed into my mind as if it had waited for me there.' Later, *The Road from Colonus,* 'hung ready for me in a hollow tree not far from Olympia'. But a third story, *The Rock,* though equally inspired, was thoroughly bad: 'My inspiration had been genuine but worthless, like so much inspiration'. The story was not published until after his death.

## A SLOW WORKER

During his time as a novelist, Forster was mainly 'set going by my own arguments and memories', working on his material more slowly – although 'I have always found writing pleasant, and don't understand what people mean by "throes of creation."' But there could be serious hitches: *A Room With a View*, for example, was the first of his published novels that Forster worked on, but he was unable to complete it for several years, and it appeared only in 1908, after *Where Angels Fear to Tread* and *The Longest Journey.*

Forster suddenly 'dried up' after the

In Forster's world, emotional and intellectual confusion are at the root of many evils. This 'muddle' – is often caused by the conflict between conventional expectations and the true nature of the individual. Some of Forster's characters are lucky enough to be rescued by people more clear-sighted than themselves, as Lucy Honeychurch is rescued by old Mr Emerson; "there's nothing worse than a muddle in all the world", he tells her. But the muddle in Adela Quested's head, which precipitates the crisis in *A Passage to India*, is only cleared up by a moment of illumination in which her head and her heart re-establish contact.

### SYMBOLIC PATTERNS

Forster's novels are set in the real world and are convincingly lifelike in characterization, motivation and action. But they also work on the reader's imagination at other levels. In some of the novels there are dominant symbols, notably the Marabar Caves in *A Passage to India* and the old house, Howards End, in the book named after it. More subtly, the novels are full of patternings and repeated images which powerfully reinforce the overall meaning – though Forster insisted that these were not the work of the conscious mind: 'People will not realize how little

**Rural idyll**
*(right) With the celebrated composer Ralph Vaughan Williams, Forster staged the 1934 and '38 pageants in his Surrey village of Abinger Hammer.*

**The Independent Review**
*(below) Forster's early essays and stories appeared in this periodical started by ex-Cambridge friends.*

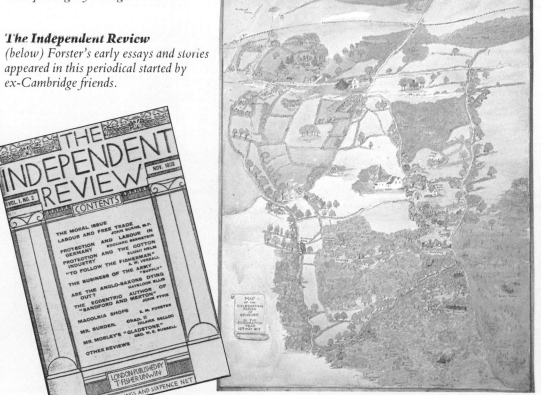

By permission of the Provost and Scholars of King's College, Cambridge

By permission of the Provost and Scholars of King's College, Cambridge

BBC Hutton Picture Library

***Speaking out***
*(left) As a member of the PEN congress of international writers, Forster denounced acts of state censorship.*

***Musical inspiration***
*(right) Forster drafts the libretto for Benjamin Britten's opera Billy Budd, premièred in 1951. The composer is in the background.*

***Indian twilight***
*(below) Forster's beloved India inspired not only his final, greatest novel but also the late memoir,* The Hill of Devi.

publication of *Howards End* in 1910. Whether or not the book's great critical success had anything to do with this is difficult to say. Then in 1913 a memorable visit to Edward Carpenter released his writing block, and he again had the experience of instantly visualizing a plot and a set of characters. *Maurice* was dashed off in three months. But, as Forster very well knew, the novel was unpublishable 'until my death or England's', which may have been why there was no further renewal of his creativity.

After the outbreak of World War I, Forster convinced himself that it was impossible to write in a world of horrors, and by 1919 he was telling a correspondent that 'I'm no longer a novelist'. To another he wrote: 'I've stopped creating . . . the scraps of imagination and observation in me won't coalesce.' He still had a long and distinguished literary career in front of him, above all as a writer of essays which constitute a superb defence of civilized values. But before this, in a final burst of creative energy, he would make his second trip to India, take up the novel he had sketched out and abandoned in 1912, and create, in *A Passage to India*, his finest work of fiction.

Gilbert Garcia/The Image Bank

# WORKS·IN OUTLINE

Among Forster's early works are some delightful fantasies later collected in *The Celestial Omnibus* (1911). His first published novel *Where Angels Fear to Tread* (1905), brings conventional England into shocking contact with old Italy, and in *The Longest Journey* (1907) convention weighs heavily.

But the atmosphere is lighter in *A Room with a View* (1908). *Howards End* (1910) established Forster as a major writer, but he published no more fiction for 14 years – until *A Passage to India,* in 1924.

Thereafter he published essays, two biographies, a popular book of literary criticism *Aspects of the Novel* (1927), and an entertaining, erudite guide to Alexandria, *Pharos and Pharillon* (1922). Only after his death did another novel appear: *Maurice*, first drafted in 1913-1914.

## WHERE ANGELS FEAR TO TREAD
### ◆ 1905 ◆

*The romance of foreign travel* (left) beguiles Lilia Herriton, a brightly impulsive widow in her early thirties. She escapes the supervision of her smug in-laws by taking a trip to Italy with a neighbour, Caroline Abbott, and promptly falls in love with a young Italian named Gino Carella. The Herritons are too late to prevent Lilia's unsuitable marriage, and she soon discovers the bitter truth about a wife's place in Italian society. Then Lilia dies in childbirth, and the Herritons make up their minds to 'rescue' the baby from Gino's clutches, never considering that Gino might refuse to sell them his child. Mrs. Herriton, Lilia's domineering mother-in-law, sends her son Philip and daughter Harriet to Italy, where they are joined by Caroline Abbot. Philip and Caroline realize that Gino is deeply devoted to his son, and decide to leave well alone. Harriet, however, is blinded by self-righteousness, and kidnaps the baby leading to a tragic outcome.

## THE LONGEST JOURNEY
### ◆ 1907 ◆

*The rough-and-tumble of a rugby match* (right) brings a turning point in the life of Rickie Elliot, a lame young man with literary ambitions. At Cambridge, Rickie meets Agnes Pembroke and her athletic, dislikeable fiancé, Gerald Dawes. When Gerald is killed playing rugby, Rickie in turn becomes engaged to Agnes. A problem arises when Rickie discovers that he has an illegitimate half-brother, an engaging drunkard named Stephen Wonham. The conventional Agnes is horrified, and convinces Rickie – despite his qualms of conscience – that the scandal must be hushed up and Stephen left in ignorance of his parentage. After this failure of integrity, things go badly for Rickie. He marries Agnes, but they quarrel when she schemes to have Stephen sent away. Then Stephen discovers the truth for himself, and later that day Rickie, too, learns that Stephen is the son of Rickie's beloved mother – not, as Rickie had assumed, of his hated father. His attitude completely changed, Rickie leaves with Stephen. But tragedy lies in store for them.

Paul Chabas: The Corner of the Table/Musee des Beaux Arts, Tourcoing: Giraudon/Bridgeman

## HOWARDS END
### ◆ 1910 ◆

*The joys of civilized life* (left) figure in this novel in which Forster investigates the spiritual condition of middle-class England through the intertwined destinies of two families, the Schlegels and the Wilcoxes. The sisters Margaret and Helen Schlegel lead cultivated lives, devoted to concert-going and good conversation. By contrast, Henry Wilcox is a businessman, successfully grappling with the 'real' world, but self-deceiving, distrustful of ideas and fearful of emotion. His children Charles, Paul and Evie, take after him, but his wife Ruth is a different kind of being. She represents an older England, and the central symbol of the book is her family home, Howards End, a farmhouse with its great wych-elm leaning over it.

The active, impulsive Helen Schlegel has the first significant encounter with the Wilcoxes, falling in love with Paul before rapidly becoming disillusioned. She and Margaret take up with Leonard Bast, a clerk with aspirations to culture. Socially and even sexually he is a victim of the Wilcoxes, and Helen, angry at the world's injustice, lets him make love to her.

Margaret's involvement with the Wilcoxes is even more direct. Before dying, Ruth Wilcox tries to leave Howards End to her, but the Wilcoxes ignore her wishes. However Margaret, impressed by the Wilcox way of life – 'a life in which telegrams and anger count' – marries Henry and fulfils her destiny as mistress of Howards End, though her relations with the Wilcoxes remain precarious.

## THE CELESTIAL OMNIBUS
### ◆ 1911 ◆

*Fauns, nymphs and other spirits from Greek myth* (right) frequently invade Forster's stories, which have a keen sense of fantasy and strike a completely different vein from that of his novels. His first collection of stories, *The Celestial Omnibus,* includes *The Story of a Panic,* his earliest finished piece of creative writing. A party of respectable tourists are struck by some mysterious dread, which it transpires emanates from the god Pan, who was considered the source of irrational fear (it is from this that the word 'panic' derives). They take flight in all directions, leaving behind 14-year-old Eustace; when the adults return they find him transformed, but their incomprehension brings about a tragedy. In *The Road from Colonus,* an Englishman in Greece comes across the place where he (like the mythical King Oedipus) can die in contentment and peace; but his daughter simply assumes that he is growing senile, and has him carried 'home' to England in spite of his protests.

## A ROOM WITH A VIEW
### ◆ 1908 ◆

*The beautiful city of Florence* (left, above) provides the setting for the beginning and end of Forster's most light-hearted novel. There are no rooms with views available when Lucy Honeychurch arrives at the Pensione Bertolini with her rigidly proper chaperone, Miss Bartlett. When the elderly Mr. Emerson and his son George offer to exchange their with-view rooms for the ladies', Miss Bartlett is horrified by this ill-bred forwardness, although she is eventually persuaded to accept. Thereafter the couples' paths seem destined to cross. Lucy sees a murderous street fight and faints into George's arms; later, on an outing to Fiesole, she has a fall and he impulsively embraces her.

Miss Bartlett carries Lucy hastily back home to Summer Street in Surrey, where she becomes engaged to the cultured Cecil Vyse, whose passion for her is aesthetic rather than physical. When the Emersons turn up again, they are as 'impossible' as ever, and George is first encountered naked at a bathing party. The part of the novel set in England has some delightful descriptions of elegant social life – tea parties, tennis (left, below) and so on.

Lucy rejects George's later proposal, but nonetheless realizes that she cannot marry Cecil. Thoroughly muddled, she is about to leave on another trip abroad when Mr. Emerson – abetted by, of all people, Miss Bartlett – intervenes with decisive effect.

In spite of the wit and fluency with which it is written, *A Room with a View* cost Forster a great deal of effort. He began work on it in 1902 and discarded two versions.

*Andreas Marco: Florence/Christie's London/Bridgeman*

*Lavery: The Tennis Party/Courtesy Lady Sempill/Aberdeen Art Gallery/Bridgeman*

## MAURICE
### ◆ 1971 ◆

*The writer and progressive thinker Edward Carpenter and his young working-class lover George Merrill* (seen together right) played a key role in the genesis of Forster's posthumously published novel about homosexual love. He visited them several times and on one occasion Merrill casually touched Forster's bottom – a trivial incident, but one that brought the idea for the book rushing into Forster's head. The central character, Maurice Hall, is a very ordinary middle-class youngster. The one thing that sets him apart becomes clear at Cambridge, where he falls in love with a fellow-student, Clive Durham. Their romantic attachment makes both men happy, but when Clive becomes attracted by women and marries, Maurice is left forlorn, realizing that he wants more than a merely Platonic relationship with his own sex. He makes desperate, unavailing attempts to be 'normal', but while staying at Clive's house, he has a strange, liberating encounter with the gamekeeper.

*Gerald Metcalfe: Pan/Fine Art Photographic Library*

*Sheffield Record Office, Sheffield City Libraries: Carpenter Collection Box 8/50*

# SUNSET OF THE RAJ

**British rule in India unified a vast, disparate continent. But inherent in that unification were the seeds of a new and independent nation.**

The year before Forster's first visit to India in 1912 saw the third and biggest Great Durbar – an occasion so extravagant, so monumentally self-confident, that it captured, in essence, the nature of the British Raj. It was staged to celebrate the accession to the British throne of George V, and he and Queen Mary travelled to India to see it. Two thousand workers laid 25 square miles of lawn, rose garden and polo pitches.

At the ceremony, the Indian Army paraded in its thousands. Bejewelled maharajahs and elephant-borne princes expressed loyalty to the British Emperor. But such a massive, stage-managed display of sovereignty concealed huge rents in the mantle of British power.

From the middle of the 18th century, India had been called 'the brightest jewel in the royal crown' of Britain. Until the year of the Indian Mutiny – 1857 – the East India Company had looked after the interests of Britain throughout half the subcontinent. The Mutiny was localized, and somewhat confused in origin, but it was carried out with savage commitment. 'Peace' was re-established by the most brutal suppression, but the shock of the revolt had had its impact. On 1 November 1858, Queen Victoria proclaimed that the administration of India had passed from the East India Company to the British Crown, the monarch being represented by a Viceroy.

Queen Victoria took an intense interest in Indian affairs, actively encouraged religious toleration and discouraged 'red-tapeism' ('alas, our great misfor-

***India's pageant***
*(right) In* A Passage to India, *Adela sees India "always as a frieze, never as a spirit" – a procession of colourful images detached from her experience. For as a member of the British community, she is in a world apart.*

R. Mackenzie: An Indian Procession/Fine Art Photographic Library

***Jewel in the Crown***
*After the Indian Mutiny in 1857 (below), the East India Company relinquished power to the British Crown. But there were those, even at the height of the Raj, who believed the Queen was risking too much by her intense interest and involvement in Indian affairs. The cartoon (right) refers to the Queen becoming Empress of India.*

tune'). But the aim of this benevolence was clear. Her proclamation stated that 'in their [the Indians'] prosperity will be our strength; in their contentment our security'. The need to heal Anglo-Indian relations was paramount.

So began a second century of domination, and the Victorians were more convinced than ever that their task in India was a sacred duty: 'our work is righteous,' wrote Lord Curzon, one of the most dedicated of the Viceroys.

The reasons why a huge nation of 350 million should allow itself to be subjugated by Britain were various and complex. Firstly, it gained economi–

T. J. Barker: The Indian Mutiny/Fine Art Photographic Library

PUNCH, OR THE LONDON CHARIVARI.—April 15, 1876.

"NEW CROWNS FOR OLD ONES!"
*(Aladdin adapted.)*

Ann Ronan Picture Library

cally from the British trading network. Secondly, the British brought distinct benefits: they built thousands of miles of railway, irrigated 20 million acres, established universities, schools and hospitals and employed hundreds of thousands of people. But thirdly and most importantly, India did not think of itself as a nation.

Apart from their religious divisions, Indians living in different parts of the vast subcontinent were divided by distance, language and varying economic fortunes. The starvation of a Bengali-speaking peasant could mean little to a flourishing Gujerati-speaking merchant thousands of miles away. But ironically, changes brought about under British rule helped to resolve such divisions.

## A COMMON LANGUAGE

Newly built railways and roads made journeys between different regions a matter of days and hours rather than months and weeks. The universal use of English that the Raj insisted upon soon provided a common language in which educated Indians could communicate their problems.

Nationalism itself originated in Europe. It reached India through Indian youth who received a Western education at the universities of Bombay, Bengal and Madras. Here they read the works of the intellectual giants of 19th-century England, such as Jeremy Bentham, John Stuart Mill and T. B. Macaulay. They then went on to influential employment in government service, law, journalism or commerce – and to political activity.

The Indian National Congress was formed in 1885, its first meeting being held in Bombay on 28 December. The proceedings specifically included a declaration of loyalty to the British Crown, so it did not begin life seeking indepen-

**Presumptuous pomp**
*The Great Durbar of 1911 (below) was a stupendous exercise in public relations, implying universal delight in British domination. But there were already those among a small, educated Indian élite who questioned the new King's right to rule.*

dence. Its aim was reforms within the framework of existing British rule. Some members did believe, however, that the British sense of fairness would eventually lead them to concede self-government, and some were in favour of agitation to that end.

The religious divisions of India were reflected in Congress. More than half the Congress participants were Hindus, including members of the strict Jain sect. There were only two Muslims, the rest being Parsees, who were Persian in origin. The Congress was therefore dominated by Hindus, which gave the Muslims cause for suspicion and mistrust.

Among the British themselves opinion was divided as to why they were in India. There was a certain line of thought which argued that the British had generously undertaken to 'civilize' this savage nation until such time as it might be fit for self-government. Another – more honest – outlook

said, 'We keep it for the sake of the interests and the honour of England'.

Victorians in England had a distorted view of India. They saw pictures of Hindu widows burned on their husbands' funeral pyres and rejoiced in the thought that the British had put an end to the practice. They heard of famine relief and felt a warm glow of self-righteousness. Meanwhile, the only Indians they actually encountered were the princes and Parsees educated at Oxford and Cam-

bridge – such as 'Ranji', who batted for England in 15 test matches, and Sir M. M. Bhownagree, who held the Tory seat of Bethnal Green.

Those British who lived in India – the Anglo-Indians in Forster's novel – had scarcely a better understanding of the indigenous population. (It is significant that Forster, who wrote with some measure of insight, was not an employee of the Crown, but worked for a Maharajah.) Officials of the Raj, whether soldiers or civil servants, were strenuously

**Railway links**

*(above) The railway transformed communications in India. British engineers and armies of Indian workers laid thousands of miles of track over wildly varying landscapes across the sub-continent.*

**Curry, rice and tigers**
*An illustrated book of the time (left) suggested that Raj life was a mixture of genteel Victorian habits spiced with adventure and novelty. In the hot season, the British would remove to the cooler Himalayan foothills (below). Tiger hunts (right) were often undertaken as family outings, albeit amid a hoard of bearers, beaters, drivers and other servants.*

discouraged from fraternizing, and there was no more despised social pariah (outcast) than the Englishman who had 'gone native' and lived with the Indians. Helpful brochures were issued to newcomers instructing them in dealing tactfully with the natives – how not to offend their 'izzat' (self-respect). But this was mere management training and had nothing to do with closing the cultural gap.

Rules of conduct rigidified every aspect of British colonial behaviour. A young government official going out to India would set foot on a social ladder as towering as any caste system. At its base was the common soldier and the 'box wallah' (civilian tradesman); at the top the Viceroy.

The newly recruited civil servant would be expected to remain a bachelor for some years before home-leave enabled him to find a suitable wife. He would work knee-deep in the welter of paperwork which characterized the stupendously bureaucratic Raj. His social life would be restricted and highly formal, the boredom broken only by hunting, polo and the summer removal.

## LITTLE ENGLANDS

In summer the entire mechanism of government moved to the cooler hills, where a succession of little Englands sprang up, complete with hunts, croquet lawns, church, theatre, gymkhanas, newspapers and libraries. By 1903, there were 1400 European-style houses in Simla, the summer capital. Simla's glorious Viceregal lodge housed state balls, and many a romantic liaison began there for wives sent alone to their summer retreats.

Under the Raj, life was empty for British women. Their children were shipped back to England to be educated – providing they had not succumbed to one of the many contagious diseases. Men could spend time at their clubs, offices, barracks or on prolonged business trips; but women had no work to do and had to confine their friendships to whites of their own status – if any lived within visiting distance.

*Dazzling Viceroy*
*George Nathaniel Curzon first saw India as a correspondent for* The Times. *He fell in love with the country and his thrusting ambition took him to the highest rank of all – Viceroy (1898-1905). With an army of 250,000 at his command and more power than most monarchs, he cut a figure larger than life – a writer and explorer as well as a statesman. Proud to the point of arrogance, he made sure always to out-dazzle the finest India could offer.*

*Master and servants*
*Households of the Raj employed huge numbers of servants – personal attendants, dhobi-wallahs (launderers), punka-wallahs (fan-bearers) and so on. So much servility (below) contributed to the 'sahib's' attitude of superiority. Many Britons would have agreed with Mrs Turton when she told Mrs Moore: "You're superior to everyone in India except one or two of the ranis [princesses], and they're on an equality."*

Contempt for inferiors was virtually a rule of etiquette, and contempt for the Indians went without saying. The British never considered that their contempt might be reciprocated.

The future politician Subhas Chandra Bose wrote home from Cambridge University, 'what gives me the greatest joy is to watch the whiteskins serving me and cleaning my shoes.' By 1927, he was a junior member of the National Congress and was advocating direct confrontation with the British Government. His lifetime had seen an irreversible change in Indian thinking.

Japan's victory over Russia in 1905, revolutions in Persia in 1906 and Turkey in 1908 had been an immense stimulus to Asian nationalism. They proved Europeans were not invincible in battle. The Sinn Fein in Ireland had also proved British rule could be challenged by force.

## ERROR OF JUDGEMENT

But nothing had a greater impact on the nationalist movement in India than a mistake made by the Viceroy himself. In 1905, Lord Curzon, believing Bengal was too large to be governed efficiently as a single province (it had a population of 80 million), ordered it to be divided. In neither of the new provinces were the Bengali-speaking Hindus – the largest single group in the old, undivided province – in the majority. They therefore interpreted Lord Curzon's action as a deliberate move to weaken Hindu-Bengali national feeling. Congress was galvanized into action.

When liberal methods such as petitions and protests failed, Congress resorted to a boycott of British goods. In 1906 it demanded that 'the system of government obtaining in the self-governing British colonies should be extended to India.' This upsurge of Hindu political activity provoked a Muslim reaction. The All-India Muslim League pledged loyalty to British rule, approved the partition of Bengal and condemned the boycott.

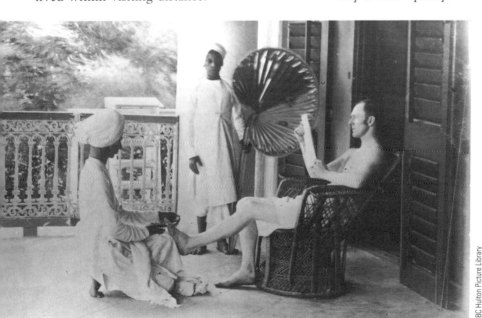

THE PARTITION OF INDIA 1947

N W FRONTIER PROVINCE
AFGHANISTAN
BALUCHISTAN
WEST PAKISTAN
Karachi
SIND
WESTERN INDIAN STATES
JUNAGADH
Bombay
ARABIAN SEA
GOA
MYSORE
TRAVANCORE
CHINA
1949 KASHMIR
PUNJAB
Lahore
Amritsar
TIBET
NEPAL
BRAHMAPUTRA
SIKKIM
ASSAM
UNITED PROVINCES
RAJPUTANA
GANGES
BIHAR
BENGAL
CENTRAL INDIA
Calcutta
Dacca
EAST PAKISTAN
CENTRAL PROVINCES
HYDERABAD
ORISSA
BURMA
BAY OF BENGAL
MADRAS
Madras
Moslem Majority
Hindu Majority
Buddhist Majority
Boundary of British India before 1947
India-Pakistan Boundaries after partition
CEYLON

*The end of an era*
*British influence was bolstered by India's ruling classes (top), whose fabulous wealth and absolute (local) power depended on no social change. They, too, were the losers when India rejected the Raj. The peaceful resistance of Gandhi and the efforts of last Viceroy Louis Mountbatten (above right) paved the way for India's Independence in 1947.*

So, by 1906, there were four major strands of Indian political activity: the moderates within Congress who wanted self-rule by constitutional means; the extremists within Congress who wanted independence through agitation; the Muslims outside Congress who wanted British protection to safeguard their interest; and a small terrorist movement which favoured assassination and sabotage as direct protest against British rule.

The Morley-Minto Reforms (called after the statesmen who devised them) were implemented in 1909, and were an attempt by Britain to make the Raj more of a partnership than a dictatorship. Morley, head of the India Office, said, 'Reforms may not save the Raj, but if they don't, nothing will.' Indian opinion was at least gratified by the re-unification of Bengal in 1911 and the shifting

of the capital from Calcutta to Delhi, former site of Mogul imperial splendour.

Any possibility of gradual political change was shattered by the outbreak of war in Europe in 1914. Congress pledged its 'firm resolve to stand by the Empire at all hazards and at all costs', believing that this loyalty would be rewarded in due course. India sent money, supplies and more than a million Indians (of whom 36,000 were killed) served as troops and labourers.

As the war dragged on, however, the spirit of resolve soured. Britain's failure to win an early victory damaged her image of military prowess. Heavy war taxes, inflation and over-recruitment in the Punjab created discontent which outlasted the War. In March 1918, to counteract possible terrorism, the Government passed the Rowlatt Acts, which allowed the authorities to imprison agitators without trial and judges to try cases without juries. In fact, these powers were never used, but the psychological damage done was irreparable. On 13 April, at Amritsar, the local commander, General Dyer, ordered his troops to open fire on a crowd of 10,000 unarmed protesters and pilgrims. No warning was given: 375 people were killed and more than 1200 wounded.

## MASSACRE AT AMRITSAR

Indians were horrified at the massacre, and were outraged by the British reaction. Although Dyer was relieved of his command, the Lieutenant Governor of the Punjab approved his action as did a majority in the House of Lords. British newspapers condemned it utterly, but such condemnations came too late to assuage Indian anger.

Too late the British Government outlined an experiment in power-sharing, with the Government of India Act of 1919. A property-owning, educated proportion of the population were to be enfranchised, and their elected representatives were to serve on the Council of State, the State Assembly and Provincial Legislative councils. But the nation was in no mood to be appeased. The first parliament elected under the new system met in Delhi in February 1921. But these first steps towards 'responsible government' coincided with a massive campaign of non-cooperation. Nationalism had become a true mass movement.

Forster wrote *A Passage to India* on the eve of these crucial events. But the novel was restricted in viewpoint, in that the majority of people he came into contact with were members of the ruling classes. He was condemned by the Indians for showing only the white point of view, and by the Anglo-Indians for showing only the Indian point of view. What he showed was the point of view of the ruling classes, both Indian and British. The movement afoot by the time of his second visit (1921) was that of the populace at large.

When Forster returned for the last time to India in 1945, he found the Indians obsessed with 'politics, politics, politics'. The world he had known was ending. Two years later, at midnight on 14 August 1947, India formally gained independence.

Popperfoto

BBC Hulton Picture Library

# BIBLIOGRAPHY

Arvin, Newton, *Herman Melville*. Greenwood Press (Westport, 1973)

Bailey, Alfred M., *Galapagos Islands*. Denver Museum of Natural History (Denver, 1970)

Baines, Jocelyn, *Joseph Conrad: A Critical Biography*. Greenwood Press (Westport, 1975)

Berthoud, Jacques, *Joseph Conrad: The Major Phase*. Cambridge University Press (New York, 1978)

Boahen, A. Adu, *African Perspectives on Colonialism*. Johns Hopkins University Press (Baltimore, 1987)

Braswell, William, *Melville's Religious Thought*. Octagon (New York, 1973)

Caplan, Arthur L., Jennings, Bruce, eds., *Darwin, Marx and Freud: Their Influence on Moral Theory*. Plenum (New York, 1984)

Colmer, John, *E. M. Forster: The Personal Voice*. Methuen (New York, 1983)

Cowan, Bainard, *Exiled Waters: Moby-Dick and the Crisis of Allegory*. Louisiana State University Press (Baton Rouge, 1982)

Curtin, Philip D., ed., *Africa Remembered: Narratives by West Africans from the Era of the Slave Trade*. University of Wisconsin Press (Madison, 1967)

Dowling, David, *Bloomsbury Aesthetics and the Novels of Forster and Woolf*. St Martin's Press (New York, 1985)

Duban, James, *Melville's Major Fiction: Politics, Theology and Imagination*. Northern Illinois University Press (DeKalb, 1983)

Finkelstein, Bonnie B., *Forster's Women*. Columbia University Press (New York, 1975)

Fleishman, Avrom, *Conrad's Politics*. Johns Hopkins University Press (Baltimore, 1967)

Ford, Ford Madox, *Joseph Conrad*. Hippocrene (New York, 1965)

Gould, Stephen J., *Ever Since Darwin: Reflections in Natural History*. W. W. Norton (New York, 1979)

Herbert, T. Walter, Jr., *Moby Dick and Calvinism*. Rutgers University Press (New Brunswick, 1977)

Hickin, N. E. *Animal Life of the Galapagos*. State Mutual Book and Periodical Service (New York, 1980)

Hohman, Elmo P., *The American Whaleman*. Richard S. Barnes (Evanston, 1928)

Holbrook, David, *Evolution and the Humanities*. St Martin's Press (New York, 1987)

Howard, Leon, *Herman Melville: A Biography*. University of California Press (Berkeley, 1981)

Howarth, David, *Tahiti: A Paradise Lost*. Viking Press (New York, 1984)

Ingram, Edward, *In Defence of British India*. Biblio (Totowa, 1984)

Irvine, William, *Apes, Angels and Victorians: The Story of Darwin, Huxley and Evolution*. University Press of America (Lanham, 1983)

Jean-Aubrey, G., *Joseph Conrad in the Congo*. Haskell (Brooklyn, 1972)

Keesing, Felix M., *The South Seas in the Modern World*. Octagon (New York, 1972)

Land, Stephen K., *Challenge and Conventionality in the Fiction of E. M. Forster*. AMS Press (New York, 1987)

Leasdor, James, *The Red Fort: The Story of the Indian Mutiny of 1857*. Macmillan (New York, 1982)

Livingstone, David N., *Darwin's Forgotten Defenders: The Encounter Between Evangelical Theology and Evolutionary Thought*. Eerdmans (Grand Rapids, 1987)

Lovejoy, Paul E., *Transformations in Slavery*. Cambridge University Press (New York, 1983)

Miller, Jonathan, *Darwin for Beginners*. Pantheon (New York, 1982)

Morel, E. D., *Great Britain and the Congo*. Fertig, Howard (New York, 1969)

Murfin, Ross C., ed., *Conrad Revisited: Essays for the Eighties*. University of Alabama Press (University, 1985)

Mushabac, Jane, *Melville's Humor: A Critical Study*. Shoe String Press (Hamden, 1981)

Nwulia, Moses, *Britain and Slavery in East Africa*. Three Continents (Washington, 1975)

Simpson, David, *Fetishism and Imagination: Dickens, Melville, Conrad*. Johns Hopkins University Press (Baltimore, 1982)

Stone, Wilfred, *The Cave and the Mountain: A Study of E. M. Forster*. Stanford University Press (Stanford, 1966)

Summers, Claude J., *E. M. Forster*. Ungar, Frederick (New York, 1987)

Wilde, Alan, *Critical Essays on E. M. Forster*. G. K. Hall (Boston, 1985)

Young, Robert M., *Darwin's Metaphor: Nature's Place in Victorian Culture*. Cambridge University Press (New York, 1985)

# INDEX